Charles Augustus Stoddard

Cruising among the Caribbees

Summer days in winter months

Charles Augustus Stoddard

Cruising among the Caribbees
Summer days in winter months

ISBN/EAN: 9783744736343

Printed in Europe, USA, Canada, Australia, Japan

Cover: Foto ©Andreas Hilbeck / pixelio.de

More available books at **www.hansebooks.com**

CRUISING AMONG THE CARIBBEES

SUMMER DAYS IN WINTER MONTHS

BY

CHARLES AUGUSTUS STODDARD

Author of "Across Russia," "Spanish Cities," "Beyond the Rockies"
Editor of "The New York Observer"

ILLUSTRATED

NEW YORK
CHARLES SCRIBNER'S SONS
1895

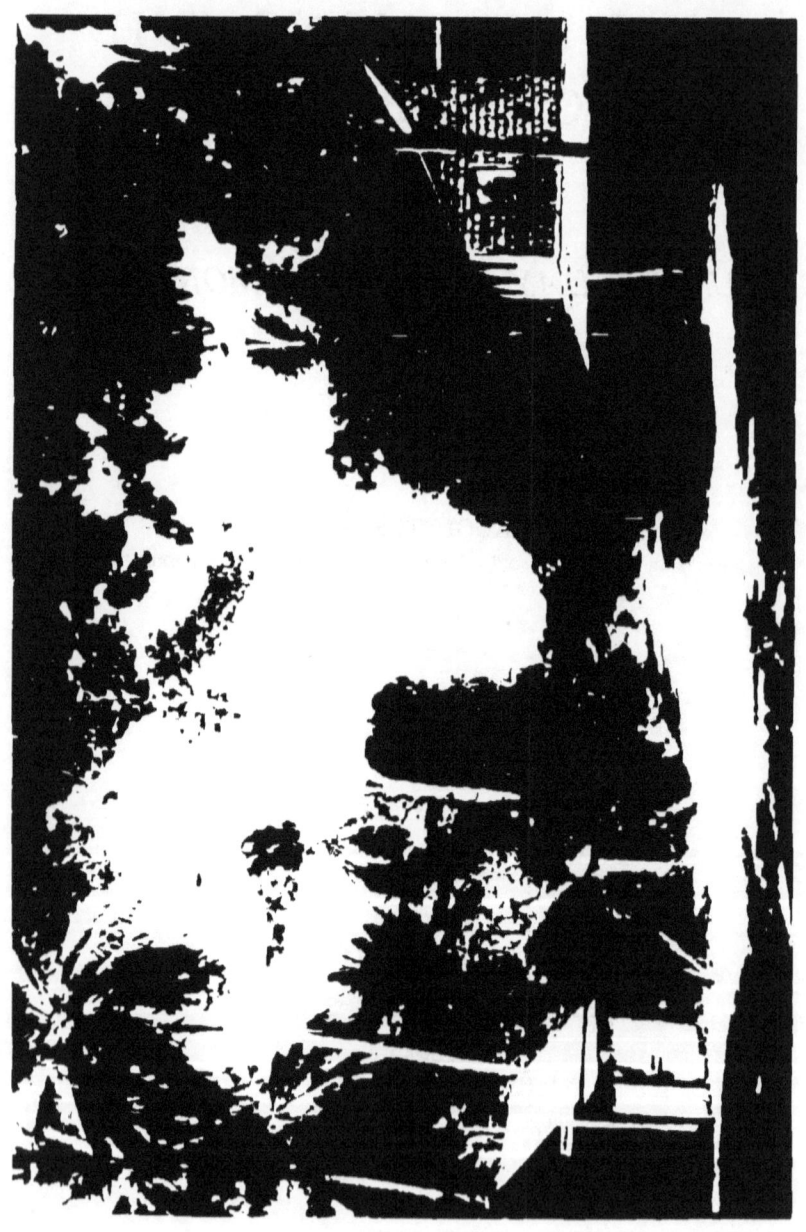

TO
IRENE STODDARD HOFFMAN
WHO AS DAUGHTER, WIFE, AND MOTHER
ADORNS THREE HONORED NAMES
THIS RECORD OF TRAVEL
IS AFFECTIONATELY INSCRIBED
BY THE AUTHOR

CONTENTS

I. LITERATURE OF THE ISLANDS
PAGE

Seeking for Knowledge in Libraries — Père Labat and his Chronicles — Hunt Collection of Books on the West Indies — Ober's Works — Kingsley's "At Last" 1

II. DISCOVERY AND CHARACTERISTICS OF THE CARIBBEES

Voyages of Columbus — Where and what the Caribbees are — Volcanic and Coral Origin — The People and their Destiny   7

III. A SEA CHANGE

New York in a Snowstorm — A Ship with a History and an Adventurous Captain — Rare Company — Outsailing a Blizzard — From Winter to Summer — Ship Island 14

IV. THE VIRGIN GROUP

The Danish Island of St. Thomas — How the United States lost it — War Vessels of Many Nations — Black Divers and Sharks — Human Beasts of Burden 23

V. ST. THOMAS AND ITS PEOPLE

Landing under Difficulties — Strange Fruits and Shells — Tobacco, Cigars, and Spirits — Dominant Races — Religion, Work, and Wages in St. Thomas 32

VI. Santa Cruz

Coldest Day for Years — Drinking Fresh Cocoanuts — Sugar Cane Plantations — How Sugar is made by a New Englander — On board the Cruiser *New York* 41

VII. From Saba to St. Kitt's

Bottom on Top — Ship building on a Mountain — A Pennsylvania School Ship — Mount Misery and Monkey Hill — Wonderful Fishes — Banyans and Palmistes 51

VIII. Life on St. Kitt's

The Aborigines, the Settlers and their Wars — Churches of St. Kitt's — A Story of Deaf Mutes — Photographs, Coins, and Curios — A Drive around the Island and a Negro Wedding 60

IX. A Real West Indian Island

Beauties of Sea and Shore — Drowsy Old Town — In Days of Auld Lang Syne — A Fountain of Youth — Birthplace of Hamilton and Marriage Place of Nelson 68

X. Antigua and its Annals

Montserrat and its Lime Juice Factory — Praying for Rain — A Tale of Abduction, Jealousy, and Death — Indian Warner — Turtle Soup here and in London 76

XI. Witchcraft and Superstition

Ignorance and Credulity of the Negroes — Obeah, what it is and how practised — Similar Beliefs in Other Nations — Anansi, Jumbee and Duppy Stories — Spiritualism and Hypnotism 86

XII. GUADELOUPE

Up Salt River — Hurricane Work — A Great Steaming Volcano — Coffee Plantations and Culture — Brilliant Market Scene — Extracts from Père Labat...................... 96

XIII. SABBATH DAY ISLAND

Rainbows among the Groo-groo Palms — Monsieur Cockroach and his Man Isaac — A Rare Mountain Ride — Tropical Airs, Sights, and Sounds — A New Paradise with Some Snakes — History of Dominica........................ 108

XIV. CARIBS OF DOMINICA AND ST. VINCENT

Columbus and the Caribs — A Forgotten Language — The Remnant of a People — Jenny the Monkey and her Reflections 119

XV. ISLE DE MARTINIQUE

France in the Tropics — Fountains and Flowing Waters — Mardi Gras and Wild Revelries — The "Swizzle" and its Uses — Snake Stories — Empress Josephine, her Early Life here and her Statue — Madame de Maintenon 126

XVI. BATTLES AMONG THE ISLANDS

Buccaneers of the Spanish Main — Count de Grasse and Admiral Rodney — A Decisive Naval Battle — The Sloop of War *Diamond Rock* 145

XVII. ST. LUCIA

The Best Landing Place in the Caribbees — Town of Castries — The Lofty and Weird Pitons — Tales and Traditions ... 151

XVIII. ST. VINCENT AND THE GRENADINES

A Superb Amphitheatre — Outburst of a Volcano — Making Arrowroot — Bargaining for a Baby — A Little Archipelago 159

XIX. BARBADOS

A Scene of Busy Life — Swarms of People — Bridgetown and the Ice House — Crisis in the Sugar Trade — Beneficent Effects of British Rule 167

XX. TRINIDAD

The Dragon's Mouth and the Gulf of Paria — Discovery by Columbus — Three Fearful Fires — Railways, Steamships, and Active Commerce — Famous Gardens 176

XXI. HINDUS AT TRINIDAD

Contrast of Races — Coolie Apprenticeship, Labor, and Life — A Collection of Living Curiosities — Hindu Priest, Accawai Indians, and Coolie Belle......................... 184

XXII. LA BREA AND THE PITCH LAKE

Where the Pitch comes from — Blackness of Darkness — Turning Pitch into Gold — Homeward Bound — *Au Revoir* 192

LIST OF ILLUSTRATIONS.

A ROAD IN THE CARIBBEES, TRINIDAD . . . *Frontispiece*

	FACING PAGE
ST. THOMAS	32
SUGAR CANE PLANTATION	46
BASSE TERRE, ST. KITT'S	60
PALM GROVE, ISLAND OF NEVIS	68
ST. JOHN'S, ANTIGUA	76
A WEST INDIAN TYPE	86
MILK SELLER, GUADELOUPE	102
INDIGO MAKING, DOMINICA	112
ST. PIERRE, MARTINIQUE	128
STATUE OF JOSEPHINE, MARTINIQUE	138
THE PITONS, ST. LUCIA	156
ST. GEORGE'S, ISLAND OF GRENADA	160
NELSON SQUARE, BARBADOS	168
GOVERNOR'S HOUSE, TRINIDAD	176
BARBAJEE-HINDU COOLIE PRIEST	188

CRUISING AMONG THE CARIBBEES

I

LITERATURE OF THE ISLANDS

SEEKING FOR KNOWLEDGE IN LIBRARIES — PÈRE LABAT AND HIS CHRONICLES — HUNT COLLECTION OF BOOKS ON THE WEST INDIES — OBER'S WORKS — KINGSLEY'S "AT LAST"

ONE who is bound for a region which he has never visited before usually desires some specific knowledge of it in advance, though I have met occasional travellers who declared that one great enjoyment of travel was to "go it blind," meaning thereby that the unexpected gave .pungency and flavor to their experiences. It is better to go intelligently prepared, however; for one may be reasonably sure of adventures enough in any long journey, especially if it be somewhat out of the beaten track.

The four-hundredth year of Columbus and the Columbian Exhibition gave a considerable stimulus to literature relating to the West India Islands, but after all that has been written during the past three years about the great discoverer, the books upon the islands which he discovered have not been largely multiplied. In New York one naturally goes to the Geographical Society and to the reference libraries for information, but the chief information obtainable at the former, aside from excellent maps, was in volumes published from one to two hundred years ago. Among these the work of Edwards is a standard, and the chronicles of Père Labat has been a treasure-house full of interesting accounts of scenery, animals, and people from which subsequent writers have not hesitated to enrich their pages. An interesting character was this Labat. He spent two years at Martinique, then in 1696 passed to Guadeloupe where he established a station of the Dominican Order, with which he was connected, and distinguished himself as an agriculturist and an engineer. Returning to Martinique, he became *procureur-général* of the mission, and was held in high esteem by successive governors for his diplomatic and scientific services. He explored the archipelago of the Antilles, founded in the year 1703 the city of Basse-Terre, and in the same year made himself felt in the conflict with England for possession of the island.

He tried hard to convert the Caribs. They were ready to sell their secrets of healing and of poison, and to accept Christianity and be baptized for French brandy or money that would buy it, but there was no connection in their minds between religion and morality. He records his acquaintance with the Carib queen of Dominica, a woman of a strange history among the French and English, more than a hundred years old and with a large number of descendants. She was naked and bent double, but the French Father made her talk, and they exchanged gifts.

A visit to the Mercantile Library at Clinton Hall, which is one of the most wide-awake and useful institutions in the city, revealed the fullest catalogue of books upon the West Indies. There were to be found here Charles H. Eden's "West Indies," and Bates's "Central America," and the "Cruise of the Falcon," by Knight, and Charles Kingsley's "At Last" — all London books — and McQuade's "Cruise of the Montauk," a rollicking tale of a yachting trip, published in New York ten years ago, and two capital books by F. A. Ober. The last of these is called "In the Wake of Columbus," and is a record of the author's experiences in visiting the West Indies to solicit the co-operation of the various governments of the islands in the World's Fair at Chicago. A previous visit to the West Indies a dozen years before had qualified Mr. Ober for such an embassy, in which he was measurably successful, as all visitors to the departments at the Fair relating specially to Columbus will remember. Besides these books, there is Lafcadio Hearn's delightful "Two Years in the French West Indies," pervaded throughout with the dreamy and delicious atmosphere of the islands, and Paton's "Down the Islands," a veritable guide-book in a most agreeable disguise. Further researches produced a list of the names of English and French works, and reference to a variety of magazine articles through fifty years; but the former were not to be had or consulted here, and the latter were chiefly of that impressionist style of literature which every child of the pen can create for himself and his transient readers; pleasant reading which is by no means to be despised, but not valuable to the knowledge seeker.

After my return from voyaging among the Caribbees, I found at the Public Library in Boston the Hunt collection of books, maps, and charts upon the West Indies. This is one of the most complete collections in existence; of great service to the traveller, and of especial use to the student of African slavery and emancipation.

Mr. Ober's book is perhaps the most useful and instructive book for the tourist who wishes to camp and hunt in the various islands. He has visited and described more of the Caribbees than any modern writer. He is an enthusiastic naturalist, and was specially devoted to birds and woods, two subjects which have more wonderful illustration in a small space in the Caribbean Islands than elsewhere in the world. His visits to the West Indies for the purposes of natural history naturally led him to take an interest in the great navigator, whose trail he was continually crossing, and as special commissioner to the West Indies, he made an exhaustive examination of everything in these islands which had reference to Columbus. Mr. Ober has followed Columbus through all his voyages, writing, as he says, "every description from personal observation, and using the historical events merely as a golden thread upon which to string the beads of this Columbian rosary." His book is lavishly illustrated and decorated, and contains more than five hundred pages, of which less than one-fifth are given to the Lesser Antilles.

Charles Kingsley's book, "At Last," is one which will repay reading, even though the reader never intends to follow in his track; for it is careful and keen in its observation of men and things, abounds in truthful descriptions and vivacious anecdotes, and is the work of a thorough and conscientious scholar, whose comparative estimates are impressive and valuable. It is fairly illustrated, but art has not yet been summoned to the illustration of this part of the world, although it has more wonders of beautiful and strange scenery than almost any region of equal extent. Of geographical illustration there is no lack, and the reason for this is evident. Sailors must have complete and trustworthy charts by which to guide their ships in this age of the world. Vessels no longer creep around the coasts, and by reason of their light draught, find their way into little bays and harbors which had never been dreamed of. Now they strike boldly across wide and dangerous seas, and run equally through night and darkness and at noonday. Lighthouses and charts and steam and telegraphs and meteorological observations and reports have become essential to commerce, while art and pictorial illustration have been only the handmaids of pleasure and luxury. But a new day is dawning, the system of picture teaching is rapidly being developed, the magazines elegantly, and the newspapers rudely illustrate their articles, and erelong there will be no corner of the earth which can be read about that will remain unknown to human vision. Then perhaps it will be needless for the traveller to describe anything except his adventures, perhaps hardly these. I am thankful that the full development of the pictorial age has not arrived; for its full advent would probably prevent me from travelling at all, and would also debar my friends from taking with me what I trust will prove an entertaining tour among the Windward Islands.

II

DISCOVERY AND CHARACTERISTICS OF THE CARIBBEES

VOYAGES OF COLUMBUS — WHERE AND WHAT THE CARIBBEES ARE — VOLCANIC AND CORAL ORIGIN — THE PEOPLE AND THEIR DESTINY

It was on the 25th of September, 1493, that Columbus set sail from Cadiz on his second voyage to the New World. It was a different scene and company from that which marked his first departure. The mystery of the western ocean had been revealed, the spell of secrecy which had hung over it was broken, and the great navigator was going forth to gather the harvest which he had sown in tears and weariness. Could he have looked to the end of his career, perhaps on that September morning he would have been content with what he had achieved, and allowed others to toil and suffer and die for the fame and gold which allured him to his ruin. But that was yet far off, and the ships sailed away to the Canary Islands, where they were to rendezvous, and whence they were to make the start for Hispaniola, now called Hayti.

On this voyage Columbus had gone much farther south than upon his first one. Then, after thirty-three days of sailing, he discovered the Bahamas, and landed either on the island of San Salvador, or on Watling Island, not far distant. Now, the fleet had not been in the open sea more than twenty days before land was seen. It proved to be an island, and Columbus named it Dominica in honor of the day, Sunday, upon which it was discovered. He could find no good harbor in Dominica, and, therefore, went ashore at another smaller island, which he called Marigalante, after his ship. He had found the Caribbean Islands, which are said to be the most beautiful group of islands in the world, covered with perpetual verdure and teeming with the rarest products of tropical regions, and it is not to be wondered at, that he thought he had attained to an earthly paradise. But these lovely spots were inhabited by a fierce race of Indians. The Caribs were said to be cannibals. At all events they successfully resisted the white invaders. Spaniards, and French, and Dutch, and English, in turn, sought to conquer them. They were crowded a little way back into the forests only to issue forth again and drive their enemies into the sea. Power and civilization could not subdue, they could only decimate and destroy them. So it has come to pass, that now, after centuries of conflict, the European has worn out the West Indian Caribs. There are a few hundred of the natives left on Dominica. They are crowded into a small reservation and live upon the charity of a government which once tried in vain to conquer their ancestors.

The West Indies make a great group of islands, which, doubtless, once formed a portion of the continent of America. One who looks at their position on a globe, or studies their physical geography and natural history, will come inevitably to this conclusion. They lie mostly in the tropics, between the fifty-ninth and eighty-fifth parallels of west longitude, and contain a total area of more than one hundred and fifty thousand square miles. The greater portion of this territory is embraced in four islands — Cuba, Santa Domingo, Jamaica, and Porto Rico, but there are more than a thousand other islands. Geographers have separated this great group into four, dividing them according to their position, their size, and their relations to each other. Thus the six hundred little flat coral islands, which form the northernmost group, are called Bahamas; the four large ones named above, with some other small islands adjacent, are called the Greater Antilles; while the curving chain of islands which extends from Porto Rico, southwesterly to the delta of the

Orinoco, is called the Lesser Antilles. These are also known as Caribbean, since they lie chiefly in the sea of that name. Sometimes they are divided into Windward Islands — by contrast with the fourth group — and Leeward Islands, the former class ending at Martinique, and the latter beginning there and extending to the coast of Venezuela.

The Antilles are volcanic; earthquakes have shaken the whole archipelago; there have been eruptions of lava and ashes during this century in some of the islands; smoke and steam arise on St. Lucia, and there is no reason to suppose that there will not be eruptions again, from some of the many craters upon the islands which now seem so extinct that a colony of Dutchmen dwell peacefully in one of them. Froude says: "The islands are merely volcanic mountains with sides extremely steep. The coral insect has made anchorages in the bays and inlets, elsewhere you are out of soundings almost immediately." According to another writer, the West Indies are remains of a mountain range which at some remote period united what we now call North and South America. The islands have been repeatedly likened to Vesuvius, and the waters about them to the Bay of Naples. Charles Kingsley in explaining this resemblance, says: "Like causes have produced like effects, and each island is little but the peak of a volcano, down whose shoulders lava and ashes have slidden toward the sea. Some carry several crater-cones complicating at once the structure and scenery of the island, but the majority carry but a single cone."

The soil formed from the lava ashes is very rich, and when well watered, as it is by frequent rains in most of the islands, it is very productive. Among the articles which are chiefly raised are the sugarcane, tobacco, coffee, and cotton. Large establishments with improved machinery for making sugar are to be found upon most of the islands, though this industry has not added to their real wealth and prosperity since the emancipation of the slaves. There are fine forests of choice woods, lignum-vitæ, mahogany, and rosewood, and these forests which cling to the steepest mountain sides have a dense growth of vines and ferns and orchids, and are full of most beautiful but songless birds. There are few wild animals remaining, but a great variety of snakes, some of which are very dangerous and poisonous, multitudes of lizards and insects of all sorts and colors and character, in which the bad are pre-eminent, being represented by the tarantula spider and the mosquito. The inhabitants are a curious mixture of all European nationalities, in which English and French predominate; there are also Hindus and

Chinese, and negroes and the descendants of negroes. who have been allied with whites, but the blacks far outnumber the whites and are steadily increasing while the white population is as steadily declining. It seems only a matter of time when these islands will return, not to the Indian tribes which Columbus found when he discovered the New World, but to the descendants of a race of black men who were brought to the islands as slaves.

This future is discussed with earnestness by the English writers who have visited the West Indies, and various plans are suggested by which the evil day may be deferred. Froude says that, as to the West Indies, there are only two alternatives; one is to leave them to themselves to shape their own destinies; the other is to govern them as England governs India, and continues: "Great Britain leaves her crown colonies to take care of themselves, refuses what they ask, and forces on them what they would rather be without. If I were a West Indian, I should feel that under the Stars and Stripes I should be safer than I was at present from political experimenting. America would restore me to hope and life; Great Britain allows me to sink, contenting herself with advising me to be patient." Sir Spenser St. John, in an elaborate work upon Hayti, shows that it is a country in a state of decadence, falling rapidly to the rear in the race of civilization; and with the steady withdrawal of the pure whites from the other islands, the same results might be expected to follow. But it is unprofitable to theorize; we will go and see with our own eyes the condition of things and try to report them impartially.

III

A SEA CHANGE

NEW YORK IN A SNOWSTORM — A SHIP WITH A HISTORY
AND AN ADVENTUROUS CAPTAIN — RARE COMPANY —
OUTSAILING A BLIZZARD — FROM WINTER TO SUMMER
— SHIP ISLAND

THERE was a dense snowstorm enveloping New York on the Saturday in February when I started for the Windward Islands. As I drove through the streets to the pier at the foot of West Eleventh Street on the Hudson River everything was wintry in the extreme. The street cars had four horses, the cable road was being cleared by an enormous snow plough, the lamps at the corners were covered with great white hoods, the employees of the street cleaning bureau looked more helpless than usual as they leaned reflectively upon their brooms and shovels. By the time I had reached the pier the large flakes had formed a thick covering to the carriage and its load of luggage. A winter storm had begun which for the fury of its winds and the intensity of its cold has been unmatched in many years. On the ocean its ravages were disastrous beyond record, and even now we have not heard the last of them. The steamship *Madiana* lay wrapped in a fleecy mantle beside the wharf. She is a large and handsome, a powerful and well-appointed vessel of 3,050 tons, originally built for the English service to the Cape of Good Hope and specially adapted for cruising in hot latitudes. In 1893 she was refitted for the service of the Quebec Steamship Company between New York and the Windward Islands. What tales these ships could tell! This steamer was first the Balmoral Castle of the famous Castle line, and Carey, one of the Phœnix Park murderers, who turned informer and gave evidence against his associates, was sent on board this vessel with O'Donnell, another one of the assassins, to be deported to South Africa. O'Donnell shot and killed Carey and was returned to England and hung for his crime. The story perhaps clung to the old name of the ship.

However that may be, when she entered a new service she received a new name, the Indian name of Martinique, Madiana, sometimes also written Madinina. We have thoroughly proved her good qualities, in storm and calm, under the northern sky and the Southern Cross. She has been our home for many weeks, and a more safe, comfortable, and well-behaved ship it would be hard to find. Her captain is a thorough seaman, and his name, Rodney Fraser, recalls some of those stirring incidents of West Indian history, when Rodney the British admiral raised the naval power of England to its highest point in these waters. He has faced danger and death in his sea service and was once thrown from the yard and lay with a broken leg in a cask of oakum, while his ship sailed sixteen days to Amsterdam. There the leg had to be broken again before he could walk, and even now there is a curious swing in his gait which is not entirely due to a life on the ocean wave.

We were provisioned for a long cruise; the tanks were full of Croton water, there were eighteen tons of pure ice in the ice-house, and in the refrigerator were fish and flesh and flying fowl and butter and milk and eggs and fruit, and abundant stores of all kinds to supply the demands of a large party of healthy Americans for many weeks. From first to last the table was well furnished, and the French *chef* proved his ability, while the stewards never failed in attention and courtesy. There was no crowd in the cabins. The ship could have accommodated one hundred, but our company only numbered fifty-six, and to this fact perhaps was due the remarkable comfort which we enjoyed in a tropical excursion of such duration, where our home was always on the vessel. There were four clergymen, two Protestants and two Roman Catholics, one physician, three editors, half a dozen lawyers, nearly as many married couples, four agreeable boys and girls, several single ladies and gentlemen, a jolly set of young men, and gentlemen of leisure and of business. There were no chronic invalids nor grumblers, no Sir Oracles nor high mightinesses, but a happily adjusted and well-balanced American party bound for a pleasant cruise, wind and weather permitting, from northern frost and rigors to sunny and warm southern seas.

Under the dripping awnings we stood awhile in the wintry air saying last words, but when the clocks struck twelve the deep whistle sounded, the propeller began to churn the ice in the slip, and slowly the steamer moved out into the North River and headed towards the bay. We soon passed the Statue of Liberty, which was covered with a white robe, and ploughed onwards through the Narrows towards Sandy Hook. Half-way down the bay the huge bulk of the Cunard steamer *Etruria* rushed by us, snorting through her steam pipe, and throwing a white cataract of foaming water from her bows with every plunge into the swelling seas. Before we discharged our pilot she was out of sight, wrapped from view in drifting clouds of snow.

From Sandy Hook we steamed directly southeast, and soon began to feel the swing of the sea, which increased as the night came down. Next day huge rollers came plumping over the main deck, and now and then a wave crest mounted the upper deck and buried the deck cabins in hissing wreaths of foam. One bark crossed our track bound north, otherwise we were alone for five days upon the deep. The second night closed in with heavy weather and high seas, which increased till it was evident that we were running before a gale of wind. Had we known from what we were escaping, we should have been thankful that our weather was no worse. All day no one was allowed on deck, and the lunch table was thinly attended, but towards night we were off Bermuda, the wind moderated, the sea grew smoother, the growing moon came out, and the air was mild. Next morning the passengers were sitting on deck without overcoats, though glad to be in the sunshine, the ladies had come to breakfast, and everybody was on hand at noon. The sky was flecked with light clouds like cotton-wool, the sea was blue like the Mediterranean, and now and then patches of a yellowish brown seaweed were seen floating on its surface. All day soft winds blew, the sea grew to an azure tint contrasting beautifully with the white lace work which edged its broken waves. Evening came on with new beauties, a half-full moon directly overhead, with its evening star at hand strangely brilliant. The constellations began to change their places in the sky. The "Dipper" was far down towards the horizon, and the North Star proportionately low. We sat out late into the night star-gazing. Morning dawned like a moist June morning in England, with occasional brief showers and rainbows with broad bands of the primary colors, then an outburst of sun warm and bright.

We sat under the awning and talked and read and enjoyed the wonderful transition from winter to late spring. The air grew warmer, the ocean was a deeper blue, and the afternoon sun drove us to our cabins to put on thin clothes and pack away our heavy ones. A rich sunset crowned a perfect day. The sea was smooth, and the sun dropped from a clear sky in less than two minutes into the waves. Immediately the wreaths of mist which had been hovering near the west took on a rosy tinge, a deep green color grew around the eastern horizon, which rose upward in three distinct shades, and was edged with soft folds of delicate pink. In the west a mass of umber-colored clouds bound with flaming red light, floated thinner and thinner till they were transparent. Then the red glow faded and darkness came at once. Soon a single star appeared near the horizon, like a diamond, and the moon white as silver rose unclouded. A few minutes later there was an afterglow, as beautiful, though not as lasting, as those which gleam along the Nile; then the host of stars came out and the evening breezes began to blow. We were all on deck; a violin, a guitar, and a mandolin had found their way into the open air, and with music and song the hours passed till the cabins were cool, and it was sweet to sleep.

The sixth day came. The sun rose fair after a night of soft showers; the sea was as blue as indigo, with little white crests where the wind ruffled its surface. Schools of little flying fish, which looked from a distance like the insect commonly called "devil's darning needle," fitted above the waves, and the sunlight struck through their filmy wings. They rose from the water and flew straight forward, sometimes one hundred feet, now and then skimming the tops of waves, seeming to get a new start as they touched the water. They were not much larger than a large smelt, and their wings were about as long as a man's hand. They are nice eating, and plentiful in the Windward Islands, especially at Barbados.

Soon after noon we began to see the dim outline of steep and high hills on the southern horizon.

Gradually they became clearer and increased in number. We could see the surf dashing high on the coasts. The lower parts of the hills were rough and rocky, the upper portions covered with vegetation and trees to the tops. No houses or structures of any kind were visible on the ocean side. St. Thomas was just ahead of us, and in the southeast were St. John and Tortola. Towards the west we could discern the outlines of Porto Rico and its outlying islands.

We scented the land as well as saw it, for the soft breeze was laden with fragrance. We kept a straight course towards a curious object which seemed to be a ship under full sail. It is known as Ship Rock, and so striking is the resemblance to a vessel under sail that one is ready to credit the story which is told of a French ship of war a hundred years ago. She was in chase of buccaneers, and seeing this rock on a hazy morning supposed it to be a ship under sail and fired a gun for her to heave to. Receiving no reply, the Frenchman laid his ship alongside and poured a broadside into the imaginary foe. When he wore ship and prepared to give another broadside the rising mist and the unmoved object showed him that he was attacking a rock and not an enemy.

The sunlight had faded away and we entered the harbor of St. Thomas under a blaze of light cast by the search lights of the *New York*, *Cincinnati*, and *Raleigh*, of the North American Squadron, which were at anchor in the outer harbor. Four ships of war of other nations were lying here, and great festivities had been going on and were still in progress when we arrived. The French admiral was giving a dinner to the officers of the other ships, and as we anchored between the *Duquesne* and the *Moltke*, their bands enlivened our evening. Many of the passengers went ashore in boats, which is the only method of landing in these waters. They strolled through the streets of the town of Charlotte Amalia, the local name of the only town on the island of St. Thomas.

We were about fifteen hundred miles southeast of New York, it was the first week in February, the thermometer marked seventy degrees as we sat under the moonlight in the picturesque and landlocked bay, the shadow of the high hills with their conical summits around us. By-and-by the youths returned from town bringing white duck suits and straw hats, in which they duly appeared at breakfast and for weeks thereafter. We were in the tropics, winter was over and gone, and in a day or two the voice of the turtle was heard in the land, and the taste of the turtle was ours to enjoy.

IV

THE VIRGIN GROUP

THE DANISH ISLAND OF ST. THOMAS — HOW THE UNITED STATES LOST IT — WAR VESSELS OF MANY NATIONS — BLACK DIVERS AND SHARKS — HUMAN BEASTS OF BURDEN

THE Virgin Islands form the northern part of the chain of Windward Islands. Columbus discovered them on St. Ursula's Day and gave them a name commemorative of the eleven thousand virgins whose bones, together with St. Ursula's, are now exhibited to credulous travellers at Cologne. The islands are mostly small, and some of them are precipitous and hardly habitable. Washed by the waves of the Atlantic Ocean which are dashed against them by the steady force of the trade winds, and by furious storms, their windward sides are rough and shaggy, and the trees which grow on these sides are so bent out of shape, that they look more like flags than trees. Yet moisture and heat produce vegetation which covers rocks and cliffs that in northern climes would be bare and ironbound. On the leeward or sheltered sides of the islands, trees and shrubs and flowers and grasses grow in profusion, and where cultivation is given to the soil it produces abundantly.

Of the Virgin group, and those which lie adjacent, St. Thomas, St. John, St. Croix or Santa Cruz, and Saba belong to Denmark; Tortola, Virgin Gorda, Anegada, Culebra, Crab, and Anguilla are British; St. Martin's is divided between the French and Dutch, and St. Bartholomew, or St. Bart as it is usually called, is French. Anguilla is a long, low, and serpentine island, treeless and unfruitful, about fourteen miles in length by three miles in breadth. It is inhabited by a population of twenty-five hundred; of these, less than one hundred are whites. The people are mostly devoted to pasturage. Several small outlying islands are associated with Anguilla in forming a British colony, which is under the general government of St. Kitt's. St. Martin's is an island of lofty mountains and broad plains, whose fertile plantations cover the meadows and hillsides, while dense forests clothe the highlands. It is divided between the Dutch and French, having about three thousand inhabitants of the former and five thousand of the latter nationality. The great industry of the place is the evaporation of salt. Twelve miles southeast from St. Martin's lies St. Bartholomew, which once belonged to the Swedes, who named its chief town Gustavia, but it is now reckoned as belonging to France.

St. Thomas, a Danish island, has an area of twenty-three square miles, little of which is level or cultivated. It lies in 18 degrees and 20 minutes north latitude, and 64 degrees 48 minutes west longitude. Its highest point is about fifteen hundred feet above the sea and it consists of a range of mountain peaks with supporting slopes or foot-hills. There are no rivers or streams, and but a single spring of water on the island. On this account, and because of its precipitous character, the soil is not tilled to any great extent, though a population of fourteen thousand live on the island. The climate is warm, there are frequent showers, and it is a healthful place and a favorite resort for invalids. This was the island which Mr. Seward, when secretary of state in 1866, bought for the United States from the king of Denmark for five millions of dollars. It was intended to use the island chiefly as a coaling and refitting station for United States ships of war. After the bargain had been completed, Congress refused to ratify it, and our government stood disgraced, and the Danish king justly angry, before the world. A glance at the map will show how valuable such a possession would be to a maritime nation, and how much more valuable to the United States than

to any foreign power. Indeed, a careful survey of
the location of the West Indies, aside from questions
about their populations, would convince any impartial observer that their proper relations and destiny
should lie with the continent to which they are adjacent. Political and social considerations modify
such ideas materially, and it is doubtful whether the
United States would now accept the outlying islands
of the continent as a free gift. That we could take
them, and govern them so as to increase their prosperity and our own ultimate wealth and advantage,
there is little reason to doubt.

We were awaked on the morning after casting
anchor in the harbor of St. Thomas by strains of
martial music, and the firing of salutes from the
French and Russian ships of war which were
anchored in the harbor. Three vessels of our own
North Atlantic Squadron, a German, and a Haytien
warship were here. The band of the French vessel
played all the national airs except that of Germany,
and we were told that on Emperor William's birthday the *Duquesne* was absent, having sailed away a
day or two previous for target practice! Yet there
were dinners and a formal interchange of courtesies
between the officers of all the ships, which had culminated in a grand ball on the night before our arrival.

Upon looking around in the morning light a

beautiful scene met our view. The harbor of St. Thomas is formed by a semicircle of mountains, which throw out prominent headlands on each side of the entrance. The mountains lie back from the sea and terminate in sharp ridges and peaks. The town is built on the slopes of three of these mountains, in the little valleys between and around the curving shore at their base. The mountains are covered with green of various shades which is formed by cultivated patches of soil and the foliage of masses of different trees. On the lower slopes white houses with red-tiled roofs are grouped, each house having some garden or greenery about it. Two large isolated structures, each with an ancient tower, bear the names of "Bluebeard's and Blackbeard's Castles." Their inhabitants are by no means robber chiefs, however, for in one of them lives Mr. Edward Moron, the very polite and hospitable agent of steamship companies which do business here.

St. Thomas is not a producing island. Its importance consists in its position as a harbor of refuge and a coaling station, and as a place for refitting vessels. Almost its only industry is the manufacture of bay oil and bay rum, for which the materials are brought from other islands like Porto Rico and Dominica, but there is a good market supplied not only with West Indian products but with the goods of many nations.

The harbor has from three to nine fathoms of water, will afford safe anchorage for several hundred vessels, and is constantly used by steamers from Europe and the United States, as well as by a great number of sailing ships and coasters. Upon our first visit, this harbor was full of vessels, besides the men-of-war of which I have spoken. Upon our second visit we found, among others, a German steamer which left New York the day after we sailed, and had put in here in distress, after battling with the elements for sixteen days, her decks swept, her bridge and wheelhouse gone, one of her officers drowned, and her hold half full of water. In another part of the harbor was a schooner dismasted and damaged, which had been blown far out of her course, which lay from New York to Maine, and found refuge away down here in the tropics. We could not be too thankful for the kind Providence which had ordered our sailing from New York a few days before one of the severest weeks in many seasons, during which the ocean was swept by fearful gales. We felt the beginning of the storm, but before it had reached its height were in the Caribbean Sea, under the friendly protection of the Windward Islands.

Before we were ready to go ashore, the steamer was surrounded with boats manned by negroes who were eager to secure us as passengers, and by canoes and boxes, from which naked dark-skinned youths were begging to dive for silver coins. This novel method of begging proved very successful, and the sides of the ship were lined with passengers eager to part with small coin. No sooner did the coins touch the water, than the divers would plunge out of their frail craft, and follow them down rapidly, getting beneath the sinking coins and soon reappearing with them in their hands. These black divers paid no heed to the huge sharks which we could plainly see swimming about the ship, and seemed to enjoy entire immunity from them. Sometimes several divers would plunge after a single coin and contend beneath the surface for its possession, remaining under water for so long a time that we thought they would surely be drowned. At last they would reappear, the victor holding the coin high above his head, and the whole group puffing and blowing like a school of porpoises. All day they haunted the steamer, calling to those who looked over the rail: "Father, throw a sixpence to your son;" "Massa, see your boy dive for one shilling;" "Now, missis, see I not 'fraid shark, down I go." At nearly all the islands similar black divers surrounded the vessel, and afforded great amusement by swimming races and diving under the keel, as well as by catching coins before they could reach the bottom. As the water was often so clear that the bottom could be seen at a depth of seven fathoms, their movements could be plainly traced beneath the surface.

Before going ashore at St. Thomas some of the party rowed over beyond the huge dry dock, to see the women dumping coal from a large British steamer which had just arrived with a cargo. The vessel was alongside a jetty, and a wide gang-plank had been rigged from its deck to the pier. Two files of women passed up and down this plank constantly, one line bearing baskets containing a hundred pounds of coal on their heads down the plank, and the others balancing the empty baskets as they walked up to have them filled. They walked from the hips, keeping the body perpendicular, and sang a sort of a rhythmical chant as they stepped swiftly along to the dumping ground. Black, rough, coarse in face and feature beyond description, they seemed like huge human beasts of burden. With long arms, great prehensile hands and fingers, large, misshapen, and unshod feet, with dirty turbans on their heads, bare breasts, and rags half concealing their nakedness, they marched up and down the planks for hours, a weird and disgusting spectacle. The pay is prompt and good, and many women and girls earn a living for the family by this hard and dirty work. They become rude and vulgar as the natural consequence of such an employment, and when work is done they are ready for a drinking bout or a satyr's dance. But in these tropical countries negro men and women do all the work, and do it under the most primitive, difficult, and disagreeable conditions.

V

ST. THOMAS AND ITS PEOPLE

LANDING UNDER DIFFICULTIES — STRANGE FRUITS AND SHELLS — TOBACCO, CIGARS, AND SPIRITS — DOMINANT RACES — RELIGION, WORK, AND WAGES IN ST. THOMAS

THERE are no piers or wharves at any of the ports in the Windward Islands, except at St. Lucia. Freight is, therefore, put on board or removed in lighters, and passengers and their luggage are transferred in most cases by means of rowboats. At St. John's on the island of Antigua and at Port of Spain on Trinidad this service was performed by a steam launch. With these exceptions, the black boatmen had to do the transportation, and very eager they were to get the job. But for the forethought of the steamship company and the attention of its officers we should have been the prey of a howling mob of boatmen, to whom the wild Arabs of Tangier would have been as tame as sucking doves. Each passenger was furnished with boat tickets, and the purser and his aids summoned the boats in order and determined how many each should carry. In spite of these preliminaries and limita-

ST. THOMAS

tions, embarkation either in going or coming was of the nature of pandemonium and purgatory. Each boatman would seek to get the bow of his boat nearest the gangway or staircase which hung alongside the ship, and as there was often a swell and always the chance of tumbling overboard, these scenes were sometimes exciting. Yelling and screaming, pushing and pulling, vociferating the names and attractions of their boats, and abusing one another in the grossest language, the half-naked negroes struggled and bid for passengers. When once these were obtained, the tempest of words ceased, and the oarsmen pulled with perfect good-nature and much deliberation to the landing-place. But though the boatmen ceased to quarrel, they never ceased to chatter and to either laugh or sing. Some travellers have spoken of the silence and melancholy of the black races. These quietists do not live in the West Indies; the whole population chatter and laugh and make a noise all the time that they are awake, and the language which they use at most of the islands, in talking with each other, is utterly unintelligible to the ordinary linguist. They speak English to the visitor or tourist in all the islands except those which belong to France, and understand him in his own tongue, but between themselves they have a jargon curiously compounded.

Morning had not fully dawned before a fleet of small boats, with from one to three negroes, clustered around the steamer. From these boats certain privileged women came on deck and established a bazaar under the awning, where they displayed oranges, bananas, green cocoanuts, sugar-cane, sapodillas, and other fruits, together with skull-caps, mats, and bags made of shining seeds, and strings of red and white beans, and other West Indian curiosities, which were tempting to the eye. In the boats were fruits and shells, and long branches of coral and palm tree canes, all of which were offered at such low prices that the passengers were soon well supplied.

We landed at St. Thomas in front of a little square which was overhung with palm and mango trees, and also shaded by lofty ferns, and were at once among a strange population. A few white men, standing here and there, were entirely swallowed up by the crowd of black, brown, and yellow men and women. The clothing of the crowd was brilliant in color, but scanty in amount, the men wearing little save short trousers and an old straw or felt hat, and the women a single robe of dirty white or pink, looped up to the knee, with a turban made from a gaudy bandanna handkerchief on the head. The children were all dressed in black, just as nature made them, with eyes that shone like glass beads, and white ivory teeth that gleamed and smiled all the time as they ran or tumbled about. Some of the women were carrying trays full of vegetables, fruit, bread, or small wares upon their heads; others were squatting upon their heels, while in front of them were little piles of sweet potatoes, peppers, limes, or a few sticks of sugar-cane; others again were hawking strings of shells and shining beans called "Job's tears," or pieces of coral and sweet cakes. The town of Charlotte Amalia is mostly built along one street which curves with the shore, and there is a road in each direction beyond the shops. The red tiled roofs of white houses rise in regular gradations from the business street for some distance up the mountain side, so that the view from the water is picturesque. If one climbs to the hill above the town, he obtains a charming picture, of which the high-colored villas form the foreground, the beautiful bay, with its ships and little islands, occupies the middle distance, while beyond, across the blue sea, are the shadowy forms of other islands like Santa Cruz and Porto Rico.

The island of St. Thomas belongs to Denmark, but if it were not for the fact that there is a little band of Danish soldiers here, that the Danish flag is hoisted on the public buildings and the dilapidated fort, and that one gets change for American dollars in money that is current nowhere else, even among diving boys, this ownership might pass unheeded. The business seems to be done largely by English, Spanish, and Jews; there is, as I have remarked, little planting and much importing; there is said to be also a good deal of smuggling from the island to the United States, of tobacco, cigars, and spirits. Certainly the cigars which come into St. Thomas without duty offer a temptation to smugglers. The best Cuban cigars, which sell in New York for seventeen and twenty dollars a hundred, were purchased by some of our party for eight and ten dollars, and we bought delicious bay rum at twenty cents a bottle, which costs three or four times as much in the United States.

The population of St. Thomas is about fifteen thousand, and they are mostly black. We began to see at once the fact, which was impressed upon us more and more forcibly at each island, that black people inhabit the West Indies, and that the great majority of these black people are negroes. There are mixed races which have been formed by the union of white and colored people, but the black effaces the white, and in general where there has been negro blood in the alliance it dominates in the result. Black people everywhere formed the rule, with white people now and then as exceptions. But yet the whites are the rulers and magnates. They chiefly own the estates or manage them for absentee owners, they are the agents and shippers, and they usually bear themselves with the pride of a conscious superiority towards the other races. I say races, for in some of the islands there are Caribs, and Hindus, and Chinese, besides the Creole descendants of English and French and Spanish people. As for religion, the Roman Catholic faith pervades the islands. In the English possessions there is always a Church of England, which embraces the English planters and their attorneys, and a few of the West Indians and negroes; also a Wesleyan Methodist church, which is nearly, if not quite, composed of black members with a black pastor. Both of these churches are well supported in British islands, but the masses of the people everywhere are Roman Catholics. In the French islands the exceptions are not worth mentioning, and in all, the influence of the priests over the colored people is great, and usually beneficent. They exhort them to industry, and faithfulness in their relations to each other; they urge marriage, it must be said with small success so far as the legal and ceremonial contract is concerned, but there is much fidelity really practised without oath or promise.

I had heard a great deal of the indolence of the

negroes in the West Indies. I saw little. Taking into consideration the low pay for labor — from four cents a day, in Barbados, to a shilling or thirty cents a day in the best labor market of the islands — and considering also climate and the possibility of easy existence without laboring, it seemed to me that the negroes were an industrious class of people. They are very strong, and use their strength without stint; they have few resources when they are not actually at work, and hence they lounge about or lie in the sun, and chatter and laugh immoderately; but on the plantations, in the sugar-houses, in the loading and unloading of vessels, as porters and servants, and in all menial employments, they appeared as industrious, and far more faithful than the high-priced laborers of New York City or of the farming regions of America with which I am acquainted. For downright, wicked laziness the full-paid employee on the public works of New York City can beat any West Indian negro out of sight. The negroes are not thriftless either. The savings banks in the islands are full of their deposits. In St. John's, Antigua, the savings bank holds forty thousand pounds. One-quarter of this belongs to negroes, and out of nineteen hundred depositors they represent more than one-half. This is but an example of what is true of other islands also.

Most of the white people have come to the West Indies to make a fortune and intend to return to Europe or America to spend it; they are not careful to contribute to the interests of their temporary home, except so far as these bear upon their ultimate prosperity. To this fact is due in a large degree a deterioration of morals and personal character among the black people, who are naturally imitative and are powerfully influenced by the superior race; but they are very much better than they have been portrayed by careless and often immoral writers and travellers.

St. Thomas has a public library and hospital, few sights except the robber castles and the house where Santa Anna lived when he was banished as a traitor from Mexico; and its great interest centres in the arrival and presence of ships of war, for which it is a favorite winter resort, and of other vessels which put into the port for repairs. It had given us our first taste of life in the Caribbean Islands, and we were ready for new experiences. Laden with bay rum, and island postage stamps, which had a boom at the time of our visit, with Carib baskets filled with green cocoanuts, sapodillas, soursops, green oranges of delicious odor, and bunches of tiny bananas, we made our way back to the *Madiana*. The cargo had been unloaded, the hatches were on, and at four o'clock the anchor was out of its bed, the vessel had swung around and was headed for Santa Cruz, which could be dimly seen upon the horizon forty miles away due south. The rich green of the mountain deepened to purple as we moved out of the harbor, the picture of the town gradually diminished till it was like a view from the wrong end of an opera glass, and the war-ships became white dots on the black water. More and more faint the outline of St. Thomas faded as the sun dropped, and night came quickly, recalling the oft-quoted lines of Coleridge's "Ancient Mariner":—

> "The sun's rim dips, the stars rush out,
> At one stride comes the dark."

Then the moon appeared, clear and full, and all the sea glowed in her silver light. A gentle breeze ruffled the waters, the air was pure and balmy, and we were in a region of terrestrial delight.

VI

SANTA CRUZ

COLDEST DAY FOR YEARS — DRINKING FRESH COCOANUTS — SUGAR CANE PLANTATIONS — HOW SUGAR IS MADE BY A NEW ENGLANDER — ON BOARD THE CRUISER NEW YORK

SANTA CRUZ is but a few hours' sail from St. Thomas, and there are schooners which taking advantage of the trade winds make the run back and forth several times a week. We left St. Thomas between four and five o'clock and by eight had made the run of forty miles and cast anchor in the roadstead. Santa Cruz is the largest of the Virgins, being twenty-five miles long and five miles wide. It sustains a population of about twenty-five thousand, and though the island belongs to Denmark the people speak English, and give no signs of their nationality beyond their little garrison and its flag. As soon as the anchor was down, the young men of the party went ashore. They returned with glowing accounts of a dramatic festival which they had attended in a Moravian church, where amateurs were entertaining five hundred people in a building designed for three hundred. As the waits were long and both actors and audience were negroes, the atmosphere soon became intolerable for the New Yorkers. They had seen and heard enough, however, to awaken our curiosity and they brought back a band of negro minstrels in a boat, who made night hideous. The next morning was an epoch in the history of the island. The thermometer marked sixty-seven degrees at eight o'clock. This is unprecedented for Santa Cruz, where during the winter the mercury usually ranges from seventy-six degrees to eighty-two degrees, and the climate is very equable. The oldest inhabitant — I regret that I failed to obtain his age — declared that it was the coldest winter day for many years, and he feared that they would have snow! We had just read a meagre telegram from New York, which stated that there was a blizzard there with thermometer several degrees below zero; so buttoning up our linen jackets, we thanked God that we were not in New York but amid the winter scenes of the West Indies.

By daylight the island of Santa Cruz seemed most attractive. It is not so abrupt and severe as some of its associates, though it bears abundant evidences of volcanic origin. It consists of a multitude of little peaks and rounded hills, with ravines and valleys between them, and trends off towards the south into lowland plains and a tongue of land and sands. The mountains, where uncultivated, are colored a bluish green, but where the sugar-cane is largely grown, the color of the country is so light and rich a green that it seems as if opening spring had just spread her mantle over the land. Yet the cane is all ready to be cut, and we saw loads of it being carted to the mills. The colors of hillsides and savannas are beautifully contrasted on this island; there are long avenues of cocoa palms, with trunks rising fifty feet like polished marble shafts, and then bursting out into a miracle of waving foliage and nests full of golden-green cocoanuts. I offered a negro boy a sixpence, and he at once "shinned" up the smooth pillar and brought me down two of the great green globes. I opened one end with my knife and drank a delicious, cool draught of sweet and juicy liquid. It was neither water nor sirup; it was simply "the milk in the cocoanut"!

There are two towns on the island, Frederikstad and Christiansted, which are not known by these names, but are generally called "West End" and "Basse End." Our view of Frederikstad from the vessel had prepared us for a beautiful place. It has some buildings with arched fronts and many white and pink and yellow houses, half hidden among strange tamarind and palm and mango trees, but when we got ashore the vision vanished. The arcades were clumsy and crumbling and dirty; the streets unpaved and irregular, and the cabins where the negroes lived were far from picturesque. Throughout the islands these cabins are small and inexpensive, and often dilapidated and ruinous in the extreme. The shanties which are built along the lines of new railroads in the United States for workmen, are nicer than the majority of these negro houses. They are built of wood, and usually consist of one or two rooms, in which a large family is huddled at night. The people spend most of the daytime out of doors, and meals are prepared in the open air. There is no glass in the windows and wooden shutters serve to keep out the wind and rain. The foundations are rarely more than a few posts or large stones. A tempest would easily overturn these cabins, and they are placed so near together in the towns that a fire would naturally burn a great number before it could be put out. When, therefore, we hear that a hurricane or a fire has destroyed several hundred houses in a West India island, it is not necessary to conclude that a vast amount of property has been destroyed. The buildings serve the purposes of a shelter and a rendezvous for the family, and if destroyed, they can be easily replaced.

Santa Cruz is covered with sugar-cane plantations. They climb the hills and crown many of them, and skirt precipices, and sweep their waves of golden green down to kiss the white sea-waves. The sugar interest is dreadfully depressed now, but the plant for making sugar is here, the capital has been invested, the land has been given up to the sugar-cane culture; what can the planters do? Beet sugar, and the low price of sugar in England and in the United States, competition and hard times have joined to render sugar planting unprofitable; all the planters feel poor, while many think that they are ruined. Others, more sensible, have awakened to the folly of cultivating only one staple, and are trying to change their plans for the future; some have kept right on in spite of losses, in the hope that better times will come to help them. The emancipation of the slaves was a terrible blow to the prosperity of the West Indies, and they have never recovered from the entire revolution in labor which this change produced. The negroes are hard-working men and women, but it is after a fashion of their own. They will work only when and as they please. Such labor is unfavorable to regular production, and unprofitable where competition is keen and margins are small. The sugar question of the West India islands is one of the most serious which now confronts commerce, and it demands careful study, judicious practical treatment, and wise legislation for its solution.

Meanwhile the islands are still covered with the green fields of cane, among which run superb roads, beneath avenues of cocoa palms. Drives in the island of Santa Cruz, over these roads, led us into valleys where there were tamarind trees delicate leaved as our locust, and giants called flamboyants, leafless but all aflame with scarlet flowers; and the silk cottonwood with enormous misshapen roots and long horizontal branches, on which grew a multitude of parasites and air plants. Here, too, were the curiously formed frangipani, with hooked or claw-like branches, the banana tree with clustering fruit and its huge purple and cone-like blossom. Flowers of all colors and shapes, from the fragrant white jasmine to the yellow and red cacti, adorned the roadsides. Black pelicans floated on the sea, or sailed in long and continuous flight through the air; the groves were never without modest music from numbers of elegantly dressed birds, and innumerable brilliant butterflies harmonized in the beauty of their coloring with the superb flowers upon which they fed.

It was at Santa Cruz that we first visited a large sugar plantation. Driving on a fine hard road, neither muddy nor dusty, beneath a noble avenue of cocoa palms, which bordered fields of sugar-cane, we

SUGAR CANE PLANTATION

came in due time to the sugar mills of Bartram Brothers, one of the largest establishments on the island. It is under the care and management of Colonel Blackwood, a retired Maine sailor, who knows the West Indies and the Spanish Main by heart. After many voyages he has cast anchor here, and is doing his best to make these fields and mills remunerative. Thus far, by introducing new machinery, by keeping up with the times, and by untiring industry and personal supervision, he has made them pay, but the present outlook is almost discouraging even to such sagacious industry. The colonel showed us the processes of growth and manufacture in detail and with extreme courtesy. The cane is planted on prepared ground in wide rows, in the fall, and grows to a great height in a year's time. It must be hoed and kept free from weeds. The resemblance of a cane field to a closely planted field of Indian corn is striking. When it has attained its growth, black men and women cut the cane with a machete or cutlass, trim off the leaves and pack it into carts, which are drawn by oxen or mules to the weigh-house, which usually stands close to the mill. As soon as the cane has been weighed, it is pitched upon a moving inclined plane, which carries it up to the cutter and squeezing rollers. These seize it, and the sweet juice, colored a dirty brown, comes out beneath the rollers, and is conducted to and through a variety of strainers, and boilers, and vacuum pans, and wringers, until it appears in brightest sugar crystals, though still very brown. It is then placed in canvas bags of three hundred and two pounds each, and marked to be shipped for refining. The molasses, which is sweet refuse from the boiling, is taken off into tanks during the process and barrelled. The waste cane, called "bagasse" is dried in the open air and used for fuel. One of the labor-saving processes invented by Colonel Blackwood enables him to burn the bagasse just as it comes from the rollers. The whole of this establishment is run by steam power, and the machinery is most expensive and elaborate. Many mills are simple, the power being obtained from a windmill and the machinery being very primitive.

These mills in good times have made as fair comparative profits for their owners as the more costly ones on account of the small cost of running them, but when times are bad and competition is keen they cannot make money. Everywhere upon the islands are abandoned plantations, and buildings going to decay. This is due to many causes, among which are the absentee system of ownership, lack of thrift in management, extravagant modes of living, the unreliable character of labor. But recently, added to all these reasons has been the competition of the beet root subsidized sugar of Germany, and the low price of the cane sugar in almost all civilized countries. One owner told me that his estate and mill, which three years ago paid him more than fifty thousand dollars' profit, would this year hardly pay expenses. The islands have been so entirely given up to sugar cultivation that it will be years before they can recover from the great losses which these hard times involve, or before they can raise up new industries to take the place of those which have failed.

A New Haven shipowner, Captain Perkins, who has settled in a charming part of Santa Cruz after more than a hundred voyages to the Caribbees, kindly invited us to his house and treated us most hospitably. His piazza looks upon the turquoise sea, over which our White Squadron was tracing its course in lines of foam, as the gunboats steamed towards the roadstead; the garden was full of tropical fruits and flowers, and at the foot of the hill on which the house stood, were some of the most majestic mahogany and cottonwood and thibet trees that I have ever seen. The afternoon passed rapidly away in pleasant visiting, and before the evening gun was fired, some of us went on board of the cruiser *New York*. We were courteously welcomed by Admiral Meade and shown over the vessel by the chaplain, Rev. Mr. Clark, who is a Methodist Episcopal clergyman hailing from Calais, Me., and has been at the Annapolis Naval Academy and in the navy for twenty-two years.

Some of the party had taken a long drive and dined at a vast hotel at Christiansted or Basse End, the capital of the island, which they described as much superior in every way to West End, but the island seemed attractive to all wherever they had dined or strolled, and Santa Cruz is considered to be one of the most healthful and desirable places for residence or resort in the West Indies.

VII

FROM SABA TO ST. KITT'S

BOTTOM ON TOP — SHIP BUILDING ON A MOUNTAIN — A PENNSYLVANIA SCHOOL SHIP — MOUNT MISERY AND MONKEY HILL — WONDERFUL FISHES — BANYANS AND PALMISTES

SAILING from Santa Cruz, we came with a straight course to Saba, St. Eustatius, and St. Kitt's. The two first named are lofty cones, the craters of volcanoes whose fires have gone out. Saba is surrounded with rocky precipices. It rises sheer out of the sea more than a thousand feet, while the top of the cone is nearly three thousand feet high, and in many places quite inaccessible. The landing is effected at a rocky cove over breakers that shoot the boat towards the stony beach with the force of a catapult. Then comes a climb up a path well named the "ladder," consisting of steps cut in the rock, an ascent of eight hundred feet, so steep that visitors must be helped up with ropes over parts of the way. This difficult path leads to the town of "Bottom," which certainly seems like a misnomer after such a climb, but it occupies the level surface of a vast crater of an extinct volcano. The town is surrounded by hills, with one opening to the east, and another to the west, through which the inhabitants reach the sea. Everything has to be transported from the shore to the town on the heads of the people. Each man carries one hundred pounds up these steep cliffs, taking his load three miles with a perpendicular ascent of thirteen hundred feet. There is said to be on Saba the largest mine of pure, cool sulphur in this hemisphere. Its owner was murdered in New York, a few years ago, and the mine has not been worked since.

In the quaint town of Bottom live two thousand Dutch people. They all have fair skins and rosy complexions, with some freckles, but little tan, while there is a predominance of tow heads among the juvenile population. The whites outnumber the blacks three to one, and true to their Dutch ancestry, they are sailors and boat builders. Up in this mountain crater they build the stanchest fishing boats that sail the Caribbean Sea, and when these are finished, they lower them down the side of the mountain with ropes and launch them in the ocean. The Dutch have always been famous for overcoming obstacles. They love to accomplish what seems impossible; and here on Saba, an almost inaccessible island, where no timber grows, where there is no dock and no harbor, and not even a smooth beach, they have established a shipyard and from hence have sent their vessels built in a mountain throughout the West Indies.

St. Eustatius is a great volcanic cone, whose lip has been broken down on the northern side, the land falling away into low hills and meadow land which makes up far the greater part of the island. The island is a Dutch possession, but thinly inhabited, and without trade or importance. It was once held by Great Britain in the days when Rodney brought all these islands under English control, but it was inadequately defended, and erelong fell an easy prize to French and Dutch adventurers. In old times its caves and secret valleys served as hiding-places for pirates and smugglers, and it is not entirely free from suspicion at the present day. It is a great resort also for picnic parties from St. Kitt's, and judging from the condition in which a party returned, some of whose members paid a visit to our ship after their day's outing, there must still be stores of spirits in the crater and a readiness to share them with all comers. One of those visitors was a prominent planter who had just returned from travelling in Europe. With his "attorney," as they call the managers of the estates here, and other friends, he was determined to appropriate the *Madiana* and make a night of it on board. The captain had to be called, before the inebriates could be induced to enter their boats. They went vowing in thick and incoherent language that they would ship no sugar by a line that denied them the hospitalities of its vessels. Next morning, however, they were more sensible and apologized for their rudeness. Drinking is not done upon the sly in the West Indies. The first sign that met my gaze on landing at St. Thomas was "Rum Shop" in a conspicuous place and style, and the same name is given to the many places in the various islands where rum and other drinks are to be had. We saw abundant evidence of the effects of rum drinking, though these were mostly secondary, intoxicated persons not being numerous, except at Martinique during the Mardi Gras celebrations.

It was early on a February morning that we sighted the island of St. Kitt's, and after skirting the coast for an hour or two, came to anchor off Basse Terre, the principal town. There were a number of vessels moored in the port, among them the Pennsylvania School Ship *Saratoga*, with about ninety boys on board. They were a fine set of young fellows, under good training for a maritime life. The government of the United States is doing a wise thing in fostering this kind of education. These lads will not only supply officers for our increasing merchant vessels, but will have that fundamental knowledge which will fit them for emergency service in our navy.

When the sun rose, we found ourselves in a beautiful curving basin of indigo-colored water, which was breaking into white lines of surf upon a yellow beach. Along the beach, and for a mile inland, lay the picturesque town of Basse Terre, its red and white roofs appearing among tall cocoanut and cabbage palms, breadfruit and mango trees. Beyond the town, on gradual slopes, were many light green sugar plantations, each having a tall chimney and a group of white stone buildings in the midst. Then the mountains rose, dark green and purple in color; rugged, and broken into wild ridges and ravines for several thousand feet, till they met the sky with an edge like a knife-blade, while a pyramid of black lava formed the summit of Mount Misery. Upon this lofty peak and often upon its companion, called Monkey Hill, a mass of vaporous clouds hangs nearly all the time. In a drive around the island we once saw this cloud cap lifted for half an hour, when only

"Precipitous, black, jagged rocks,
Forever shattered and the same forever,"

stood revealed. The contrast between the emerald billows of verdure which tossed up from the lowlands, and this infernal crest, was striking and suggestive. The lava, and sulphur, and ashes, which have been cast out from the crater, and which have formed its slopes, and are still washed down to the ocean shores, have made the island fertile and beautiful. Thus the hideous ogre is changed into a fairy godmother, or in more pious phrase, our bountiful Creator is always and everywhere

"from seeming evil, still educing good."

Every morning after breakfast we landed on some of the islands, to ride or drive or visit or study the people and their customs. The struggles of the negro boatmen for the privilege and profit of rowing us ashore, became in time no more exciting than the cries and gestures of the cabmen in front of any great railway station in America; and we chose "Champagne Charlie" or "Black-eyed Susan," with supreme indifference, and were rowed ashore over the tossing waves to a long wharf and so came to the sandy beach. Here was a curious sight. Besides the lighters and gangs of longshoremen who were at work upon hogsheads of sugar and hogsheads of molasses and barrels of rum, and the ragged negroes, with ruinous carts and raw-boned horses and starved donkeys, there were the fishing boats which had just arrived with the products of their nets. These were spread out upon the sand, and a more brilliant piscatorial picture I never saw before, but such variety and beauty in a fish market I saw again and again in the markets of the Windward Islands. The fish were of all sizes and shapes, from a hideous shark to the graceful and beautiful bonita. There were the parrot fish, a gray-blue and yellow fish that looked like a drowned "Polly," with watery eye; the gar-fish, two feet long, as slender as a lance-blade, clothed in gleaming silver, and with a long black bill like a bird's, which is set with rows of fine pointed teeth; there was the butter fish, and the redsnapper, and the gauze-winged flying fish, and the beautiful angel fish, with its delicate arrangement of scales of pearl and silver and bronze and gold. Curious eels of vast size lay coiled like serpents in boxes, and there were lobsters large enough to take a small darky in their claws and walk off with him, and crabs of all sizes and colors, and forty other strange and wonderful dwellers in the sea. Dozens of men and women, squatting or kneeling in the sand, were chaffering and chattering, and handling and weighing, and selling and buying. I saw nothing but copper coin used in the purchases, and when I offered half a crown for change, in payment for two breadfruit, which cost a half-penny, there was a sensation among the dealers equal to that caused upon the Stock Exchange in New York, by a large and sudden exportation of gold.

Some writers say, that this chief town of St. Kitt's is formal, and that its population is not picturesque, but they must have seen it in rain or mist, or during a hot noontide, when the Kittefonians, as they call themselves, were resting out of sight. It is really a bright and busy town, with many neat streets of well-built wooden houses on one-story stone foundations, a handsome square containing a wonderful banyan tree, a number of fine palmistes, thibet, and other trees, and beds full of gorgeous hibiscus flowers and fragrant mignonette, and a multitude of plants and shrubs. Within the enclosures, which contain some of the best houses, are gardens full of flowers and fruits, where one could lounge under wide-spreading branches, through which the cooling breath of the trade winds finds its way from ten o'clock in the morning till long after dark. St. Kitt's does not afford such varieties of color and costume as are found in the French islands, but you will see many tall and comely women, walking with erect figure and attractive dignity which comes from carrying water-jars and other loads upon the head. The men are not all black; some are yellow with straight raven hair and eyes like black beads which indicate Spanish or Portuguese descent, but the majority are black as a coal, and look blacker still, because they are clad, if clad at all, in garments which were originally made of white material. They delight in the sugar-cane, which they gnaw constantly and vary with tobacco smoking, and they are as fond of all kinds of fruit as an Englishman is of various sorts of meat. At St. Kitt's we ate sapodillas, which have been inelegantly called "sweet mud"; mangoes which are of a beautiful color and contain a creamy substance of a slightly resinous taste; guavas, small yellow globes full of seeds and sugary pulp; soursops, a fruit like a large prickly pear, full of a substance which would be familiar to lovers of ice-cream soda, and great purple raspberries rather lacking in flavor. Baked breadfruit was pronounced a valuable addition to those products which can be used as vegetables or for the stock of puddings and other desserts, while yams and sweet potatoes, and plantains, and bananas, and all sorts of oranges, were familiar to us, though not in the profusion and at the small cost for which they can be had in the West Indies.

VIII

LIFE ON ST. KITT'S

THE ABORIGINES, THE SETTLERS AND THEIR WARS — CHURCHES OF ST. KITT'S — A STORY OF DEAF MUTES — PHOTOGRAPHS, COINS, AND CURIOS — A DRIVE AROUND THE ISLAND AND A NEGRO WEDDING

AMONG the pleasant acquaintances formed at St. Kitt's was that of Captain George Locke and his amiable wife. The captain lives on the island in the service of the Quebec Steamship Company, and he accompanied our party on the southern tour through the islands as far as Trinidad. His house is in town, but stands in a garden with palm trees and clustering vines and an ancient rose bush whose branches climb over a long veranda and adorn it, with great blossoms of the "cloth of gold." From him we gathered much useful information as we sailed along, and some of the facts about the island of St. Kitt's will be of interest before we resume our voyage. The island is oval-shaped, being thirteen miles long, from three to six miles in width, and contains an area of about forty-four thousand

BASSE TERRE—ST. KITTS

acres, three-fourths of which is under cultivation. The uncultivated part is mostly embraced in the Conarrhee hills, the precipitous crags of Mount Misery, and a long lowland stretching out to sea upon the southeast. The remainder of the island is well tilled and fertile.

The aborigines were Carib Indians, a sturdy and warlike people who inhabited the island in 1493, when Columbus discovered and gave it his name. Tradition declares that he was moved to call it St. Christopher, because one mountain seemed to him to be bearing a smaller mountain on its shoulder as the Saint Christopher is represented in early art carrying the infant Saviour. The English, when the island came into their possession, changed its name to St. Kitt's. But the Carib name was Liamuiga, "the fertile," a designation which is more beautiful and appropriate than either of the others. The Spanish discoverers did not settle here, and it was not until after the Pilgrims had landed at Plymouth Rock, that fifteen Englishmen took possession of St. Christopher. A party of Frenchmen came about the same time, and their common danger from the Caribs led English and French for once to join forces, massacre the natives, and divide their conquest. The English settled at the northwestern end called Sandy Point, and the French at Basse

Terre on the southwest. But the league thus cemented in blood was soon broken, and English and French quarrelled for more than half a century, till finally in 1690 the English mustered three thousand armed men, and eleven men-of-war and other vessels, drove the French out of the island, and exiled them to Martinique. The island has been in English hands ever since, but while Sandy Point is still a small village, Basse Terre has about seven thousand inhabitants and contains the Government House and other public buildings and a number of churches. We attended service in three, the Roman Catholic church opposite the Botanic Garden, where the congregation was almost entirely composed of colored and negro people; the Wesleyan church with a similar congregation but having more of the negro element, and the Church of England, whose services were held in a large and handsome stone structure well filled with white people, with here and there a colored person, but few if any negroes. The distinction between colored persons and negroes is very marked and is always insisted upon. Colored people may associate with whites upon terms of equality, but the negro still bears the curse of his lineage and is reckoned as belonging to a servile race.

The service at the Church of England was

conducted by a venerable archdeacon who seemed to be eccentric. He omitted parts of the service without any reason, and mixed up other parts, and his enunciation was so strange as to seem ludicrous; he smiled derisively and wagged his head to and fro till some of our ritualists in the party became indignant. But our tendency to mirth or anger was changed to pity when we learned after service that the poor rector had been paralyzed and was struggling bravely to retain his place and perform his duties. I recalled the story of the lady who had gone to Notre Dame in Paris to hear a celebrated priest. She found one chapel occupied by a congregation and presuming that she was in the right place, kneeled for a few moments in prayer. On rising from her knees, she saw that the preacher was making an address, but she could not hear a word. She tried to listen, but no sound reached her ear. Frightened at what she supposed was a sudden deafness on her part, she rushed into the main body of the church, where she met a friend, who seeing that something was wrong asked: "What is the matter?" "Thank God, I have recovered my hearing," exclaimed the lady; "I feared that I should be deaf for life." Upon hearing the story, her friend informed her that she had entered the chapel where one of the successors of the famous teacher De L'Epée was conducting a service for deaf-mutes! It is not always safe to draw conclusions from appearances, especially when travelling in foreign lands.

One of the objects of interest to the modern traveller is the photographer. Next to the pleasure of carrying one's own camera, and choosing the point of view, is that of overhauling the local photographer's stock. At St. Kitt's, Mr. Lyon, who fills this post, is a character. He has lived long in the Windward Islands, knows all their beauties and salient points, is an enthusiastic artist, and also an untiring collector of coins and curios and postage stamps. It was a curious experience to find in this far-away island some of the rarest Roman and Greek coins and things that antiquarians and amateurs long to possess. Mr. Lyon was proud to show his treasures and to share his pleasure with a group of eager travellers. I have nothing to say about the hotel facilities and accommodations at Basse Terre, except that we greatly preferred the private hospitality of the inhabitants to any public provision, and were thankful here as elsewhere, that there was a French *chef* on board the *Madiana* and stewards who knew the art of serving a meal.

In good company, I twice drove about St. Kitt's. A fine road runs from Basse Terre towards the southeast, gradually ascending from the anchorage, till the broad Atlantic with its breakers on the rocks and its far-extending billows, greets the eye. From the crest of the island the road traverses the windward shore, sometimes climbing a hill and anon sweeping down almost to the foaming waves. Running northward along the entire eastern side, a superb ocean view meets the eye upon the right hand, and a mingled landscape of sugar-cane plantations, dense forests, and ragged cliffs is upon the left. We visited a sugar mill of the simplest sort on one of these drives. The work was done by negroes, oxen, wind, and water, and the sugar which was turned out was the cheapest sort of muscovado. The owner lives in Scotland and is perhaps content with a very moderate profit upon his investment, and in these times he will be lucky if he does not pay out more than he receives, even with such primitive methods and machines.

On another drive we witnessed a marriage in the Episcopal church of St. Paul's, near Sandy Point. A large population had turned out, and the roads were so full that we inquired whether it was a fête day, and were told that a wedding was at hand. So we made our way to the church and joined the company. The bride was tall and large-limbed, and as black as night. She was dressed in white lawn, with a large necklace, made of great glass beads like pearls, around her neck, and a huge white satin bonnet on her head. A medium-sized negro girl, who also wore a white muslin dress gayly bedecked with cherry ribbons, was the bridesmaid, and the groom was a tall and powerful black man, in a gray suit, white waistcoat, and blue necktie. After the knot was tied, the party were called upon to sign the register. This operation occupied nearly a quarter of an hour, and was accompanied with much twisting of the tongue into the corner of the mouth, and difficult adjustment of the fingers so as to bring fingers and pen and page into perfect unison. At last the signatures were made, the minister got his fee, and the happy pair were driven off in a rickety coach with a raw-boned team and a charioteer clothed in white linen, followed by the cheers and blessings of a waiting crowd. They must have gone to Basse Terre, thirteen miles distant, upon their bridal tour, for this is the longest journey one can take on the island. The rector told us that such occasions were rare among the negoes, as the women preferred an arrangement in which they were left free to leave their partners, if they proved to be lazy or unkind; he said also, that those who were legally married were treated with more respect among their own people as well as by others. At the church and along the road we were met by men and girls with missionary boxes, who were collecting funds for benevolent uses, and though some doubted whether the shillings which they gave would reach further than the pockets of the solicitors, most of the party were charitable in their judgment as well as in their gifts.

On this drive we passed through the villages of Caro and St. Paul's, and embarked again at Sandy Point, where the steamer had come for some bags of sugar. There is no place to lunch or lodge on the island, outside of Basse Terre, and though the planters are doubtless hospitable enough to entertain visitors, the days when any traveller felt free to make himself at home without an invitation, have passed away. About midnight we steamed away from St. Kitt's by the light of the Southern Cross, which was now becoming familiar, and a host of other new and brilliant stars which gemmed the firmament.

IX

A REAL WEST INDIAN ISLAND

BEAUTIES OF SEA AND SHORE — DROWSY OLD TOWN — IN DAYS OF AULD LANG SYNE — A FOUNTAIN OF YOUTH — BIRTHPLACE OF HAMILTON AND MARRIAGE PLACE OF NELSON

ONE of the most intelligent and agreeable of my companions in our winter tour among the Windward Islands was Mr. Alfred M. Williams. He was one of the men who helped to make the *New York Tribune* in the days of Horace Greeley, and has since edited that able and influential New England newspaper, the *Providence Journal*. Mr. Williams is a lover of literature and of old books; a poet and an author, as well as an editor. His last book, is an interesting collection of poetical folk-lore, under the title, "Studies in Folk-Song and Popular Poetry." My friend became enamored of the beautiful island of Nevis, which he visited while the *Madiana* lay at St. Kitt's, and which I visited with others upon the return voyage. Mr. Williams has kindly given me permission to print his poetic and vivacious

PALM GROVE—ISLAND OF NEVIS

descriptions of Nevis, and I am sure that my readers will join me in thanks for his courtesy.

"The most distinctly West Indian island which we have yet seen, our port of call including St. Thomas, St. Croix, and St. Kitt's, is the little island of Nevis. It is not in the regular routes of the steamers, but is gained in an hour and a half's sail by a small boat from Basse Terre, St. Kitt's. The morning was a delightful one, the sky full of soft, fleecy clouds, which now and then darkened into mist and rain, sweeping in sheets of falling water over the wine-dark sea, and again lifting into white veils upon the mountain tops and letting the sun shine in unclouded lustre upon the sparkling vegetation and the sea, which was turned by its caress to the richest turquoise blue. The white gulls screamed with that voice which is the very accent of the ocean, as they swept about in what seemed like a madness of activity, and now and then a greater pelican would wing his heavy way above the sea. The little steamer coasted along the shore of St. Kitt's, with its high hills apparently covered with unbroken forest, and then played and rolled through the heavy waves that swept through the channel, which divides the island from Nevis. Nevis is dominated by a lofty hill, which looks down on the open roadstead. This morning it wore a light gauze veil of vapor around its summit, but down its sides there were patches of the soft green verdure of the cane fields, and the darker woods were bathed in the sunlight. As we approached the shore the white foam of the breakers was seen combing far up on the beach, and the heavy thunder of their fall gave a strong symphony of ocean music. The sea was so rough that the steamer could not approach the wharf, and the few passengers were transferred to the shore by the skilful hands of the negro boatmen.

"The town of Charlestown, which is the capital of Nevis, is a small hamlet of a few hundred inhabitants, and is hardly more than a single street, stretching along the open beach. On the sea front there is a single line of cocoa palms lifting their feathered heads high in air, and beneath them are the huts of the negro fishermen, with their boats hauled up on the beach and their nets drying in the sun. The town is made of quaint old houses of the ancient period of West Indian architecture, with mossy stone walls and tiled roofs. There are no signs of any business except a few shops of general merchandise, and an air of gentle decay broods over the whole place. There is a little public garden of a few feet square, in which roses and rhododendrons were in bloom, and around it were a few negro women with cakes and vegetables for sale.

"The white population were few, but in amends the negroes were many. Strong black wenches passed by with heavy burdens on their heads, walking with that firm, solid, and graceful step which comes from the habit of carrying burdens, with only the movement of the hips, the bust and head remaining perfectly steady and upright. All were smiling and happy, showing their white teeth, and ready to respond with a soft 'good m-a-a-wning' in the sweet, drawling Creole accent. Some were carrying baskets of bright-colored West Indian fish of strange shapes and abnormal aspect, and others great burdens of vegetables, boxes and loads of a very miscellaneous character. One would not have been surprised to see a negress with a kerosene lamp or a mirror on her head, or, if there were a square piano on the island, to see it borne with a steady step by four of these women caryatides. The men seemed to have little to do, and to be doing that without any energy. They idled on street corners and talked with a conversation heavily punctuated with guffaws, or munched sugar-cane in sleek and shiny content. Shoes, it is needless to say, were unknown, and garments were reduced to the simplest articles of necessity. Altogether, Charlestown seemed sunk in a gentle and tranquil sleep, its slumber soothed with the tranquil booming of the surf, and steeping in the warmth of the kindly sun.

"But Charlestown was once as wealthy and lively a place for its size as any in the West Indies. In the days when a plantation in the rich soil of Nevis was a gold mine, there were wealthy merchants who dwelt here, and a rich and luxurious planting population to lead a grand train of luxury and expense. Besides, Charlestown was the Saratoga of the West Indies, where all the wealth and fashion of the Windward islands gathered to spend the season at the famous sulphur baths. About ten minutes' walk from the town are the ruins of an immense stone hotel, which must have been able to accommodate several hundred guests. It now looks like the ruins of an ancient castle, so heavy are the crenellated walls of a massive gray,

'By the caper overrooted, by the gourd overscored,'

and three magnificent flights of stone steps lead up to the entrance hall. One can imagine what bevies of dark and languid Creole beauties in diaphanous muslins have passed up those steps, escorted by white-coated planters, or officers from the ships and garrisons in more brilliant uniforms, or danced and flirted in the lofty ball-room, where now the clothes of the negro family which keeps the bath are hung to dry. Only the central portion of the building is roofed, the top story of the wing having entirely fallen in, and from the walled terrace to which one climbs by a rickety stair there is a magnificent view of the town and the gleaming plain of the sea, while the soft and spicy breeze gently caresses the cheeks. It is a gentle ruin, embowered in luxuriant vegetation that has kindly wrapped and softened its decay, and is perhaps more suited to the scene than when it was alive with hilarious gayety.

"The bath-house is at the foot of a gentle declivity in front of the hotel. It is an ancient and dilapidated building, whose battered doors move reluctantly on their hinges. To get to the bath you descend a long flight of brick steps leading to a pool of limpid green water with a gentle stir and flow. It is dark, the only light coming through cracks in the shutters, and it is not reassuring to hear the scuttle of a lizard or some other beast as you reach the platform. However, you take heart of grace and disrobe. At the first step the water seems unpleasantly warm, but soon a gentle languor and a sense of infinite deliciousness comes over you. You fairly wallow in delight as you sit with the water rippling up to your chin, and you feel that you could rest for hours in absolute beatitude as the gentle warmth steals through your limbs. And when you emerge you feel as though you had never been clean before, so complete is the sense of the removal of all impurities. It is like the fountain of youth in its effects, and if Ponce de Leon had found it he would have been assured temporarily at least that the object of his long quest had been attained. Although a strong sulphur spring, there is not the slightest unpleasant smell, such as sometimes accompanies a mineral bath, and the waters are of a limpid purity. Its effects are considered very good for rheumatic complaints and stories of wonderful cures are told of its waters. It does not seem impossible that in the future, when the attractions of the West Indies as a winter resort become better known, a new hotel may arise near the old one, and that an unusual crowd of visitors from the United States may replace with their exotic ways the departed glories of the extinct Creole aristocracy. There are certainly far less attractive places where fashion resorts in search of health or to dissipate the burden of its ennui. But in that case Charlestown would cease to be a typical West Indian town and become a mere tourist caravansary like Bermuda or St. Augustine, and those who can now delight in its quaint and old-world flavor would not come to be dinned and dazed by American hotel life.

"Nevis is not one of the historical West India Islands. It was not fought for and refought for as were the other islands, when France, Spain, and England struggled for the possession of the pearls of the Antilles, nor was it a place of enormous loots, as was the neighboring island of St. Eustatius when Rodney swooped upon it. Every one will tell you that it was the birthplace of Alexander Hamilton, as they will in Santa Cruz that the illustrious Peter Jackson first saw the light there. A more famous man than either has, however, left the trace of his visit there. In the old Fig Tree church a few miles from town, the register shows that Horatio Nelson, then a post captain in the British navy, was there married to Mrs. Fanny Nesbitt, the faithful woman whom he deserted for the brazen charms of Lady Hamilton, and of whom he wrote in one of the most singular expressions of feeling ever uttered by man 'that if the Lord should remove the obstacle to their union' (meaning his own union with his mistress), as though heaven should interfere to sanction his adultery by murder. Meditating upon the strangeness of humanity, we may leave Nevis to its sempiternal calm."

X

ANTIGUA AND ITS ANNALS

MONTSERRAT AND ITS LIME JUICE FACTORY — PRAYING FOR RAIN — A TALE OF ABDUCTION, JEALOUSY, AND DEATH — INDIAN WARNER — TURTLE SOUP HERE AND IN LONDON

THE night air on the Caribbean Sea was mild and refreshing. When the passengers had retired, and all lights were out which the rules required, I used to come out from my stateroom, and spreading a steamer chair astern on the hurricane deck, recline and gaze for hours at the heavens, and at the dark masses of black mountain land along which we coasted. The West Indian night is beautiful, the sky a deep violet, the atmosphere clear, and while multitudes of stars are visible to the naked eye, the larger planets shine with a refulgence unknown in the temperate zone.

In such a night we rounded Nevis and passed Redonda, which seemed little more than a black rock, and then sailed by the lofty crags of Montserrat. This is a port of call for trading vessels, which

ST. JOHNS—ANTIGUA

receive large quantities of the lime juice manufactured here for export to the United States and elsewhere. The trees are planted closely in the orchards in order to prevent vegetation beneath from exhausting the soil. They begin to bear after three years and continue to yield well for half a dozen or more years. The limes are gathered as they fall to the ground by children and squeezed between sugar rollers. The juice is then boiled till it is thick, and if intended for shipment is run into hogsheads of fifty gallons. The juice is used as an anti-scorbutic and largely for making citric acid. It is made at other islands, notably at Dominica; but the best quality of juice known to commerce is made on Montserrat. The industry was originally established by Quakers, and it has been of far more use to mankind (and I am happy to say, of equal profit to the capitalists) than the making of rum which employs so many of the West India islanders. Many a scurvy-stricken sailor has had reason to bless the founders of this beneficent industry. Steaming slowly through the night, on account of reefs and shoals, we cast anchor off Antigua, in an open roadstead just before sunrise. When the sun rose, at once everything was bright and began to be hot. We looked upon the lighthouse on a reef near which we had sailed, and at the wreck of a steamer lying upon another reef about eight miles from shore, with the sea dashing over her decks. Masts and funnel were still standing, though the vessel had been ashore for two years and the insurance money had been paid.

Antigua is long and low, without high mountains or striking features. There are a few hills at one end and an eminence of about fourteen hundred feet not far from the centre of the island. Seen from a distance the island seemed rough and barren, but as the voyager draws near, hills and valleys open to his view, and the shore puts on an appearance of luxuriant vegetation, though destitute of trees except around the town of St. John's. This is the capital of the Windward Islands, and the governor resides here, in an unpretentious house with a public park near at hand and the beginning of a botanic garden beyond. The whole island is under cultivation and all in sugar, hence the present depression of that staple is severely felt. The want of springs and an insufficient rainfall are the only serious drawbacks to the fertility of Antigua. A story is told of a man who during a period of drought brought casks of water from Montserrat and sold the precious liquid for so high a price that he was induced to make a second excursion for water. Arriving with his cargo, he increased his figure so much that the inhabitants refused to buy, and instead united in solemn prayers for rain, which being speedily answered, at once rewarded their faith and punished his greed. The moral of the story is a good one whether it be fact or fiction. There are but two or three springs and no river, and the rainfall is less than on the other islands, yet on account of its dryness and sandy soil the health of the island is excellent.

Antigua lies twenty-five miles northeast of Montserrat and forty miles north of Guadeloupe, in latitude seventeen degrees north and longitude sixty-two degrees west. It is eighteen miles long and seventeen miles broad, and contains about sixty thousand acres. When slavery was abolished in 1834, the population consisted of about two thousand white and colored people, and thirty-three thousand negroes. Since the emancipation of the slaves the white population has steadily declined and the negroes have as steadily increased. Antigua has been the scene of a number of insurrections in the days of slavery. The island was discovered by Columbus on his second voyage, but as he found it full of Caribs, and could get no good water, he simply gave the island a name after the Church of St. Mary of Antigua at Seville, and sailed away. In 1520 Don Antonio Serrano, of Spain, tried to colonize it, but failed; a century later a French captain of a privateer made a short stay; and in 1632 Sir Thomas Warner, who is buried at

Old Road on St. Kitt's, and who was a notable man in West Indian history, sent his son with a British army to take and settle the island. There was continual fighting for years with the Caribs, who had no mind to have their possessions taken from them by Englishmen, and in 1640 a Carib chief stole the English governor's wife and carried her away to Dominica.

This raid is celebrated in the ancient legend of Ding a Ding Nook, which is briefly as follows: The wife and child of the governor of Antigua, who were very dear to him, were one day missing from the government house. Inquiry from all the neighboring planters revealed no traces of them. Gradually it dawned upon the agonized husband and father that his wife and child had been carried off by the Carib Indians. He heard that some Caribs with their chief had been seen upon the island and that they had returned to their homes in Dominica. With a few friends he sailed down the islands and landed where the town of Roseau now stands. There he learned that his suspicions were correct, and that the chief with his captives had left shortly before for his lodge in the centre of the island. He followed after, and before long found spots of blood on the path. Believing that these spots indicated that his family had been slain, the pursuers hurried forward and came upon a party of Indians, whom they slew after a severe battle. A short distance beyond the place of conflict, the governor came to an Indian lodge, and upon opening the door his wife and child fell into his arms. The blood upon the path had dropped from the bruised feet of the captives as they walked up the rough mountain path.

Full of gratitude and happiness, the governor brought his family back to their Antiguan home, but, alas, the anxiety and excitement through which he had passed disordered the mind of the husband. He began to be suspicious of his wife, and imagined that she had gone freely with the Carib chief. No devotion or affection on her part seemed able to break the dark spell which enchained him, and fierce jealousy and hate took the place of love. The efforts of friends to dissipate his fancies proved unavailing and it became necessary to separate the unhappy man from one whom he had tenderly loved and rescued from captivity, lest he should take her life. Whether the cloud ever lifted and happiness returned, the legend does not inform us.

Antigua was again captured by the French in 1656, but was restored by the treaty of Breda the next year. There was little peace for the colonists, however, for the Caribs kept up their raids till a deliverer arose in the person of Philip Warner. He was the son of General Sir Thomas Warner, the English governor of St. Kitt's. An illegitimate son of Sir Thomas by a celebrated Carib woman, who lived far into this century, had become a great Carib chief, and ruled the Indians with despotic sway. Philip determined to put an end to the Carib raids, and taking a party of men, he went to the place where his brother lived. There was great joy, says the French historian, Dampier, at their meeting. Philip made a great feast, and invited his brother and the Indians to the merrymaking, but at a given signal, his men fell upon the guests and murdered Indian Warner and all his tribe. For the murder of his brother, Philip was tried, but triumphantly acquitted, had his lands restored, and was reinstated as governor of Antigua. In 1689 Colonel Coddington, a man famous in West Indian annals, came from Barbados to govern the island. He was succeeded by Daniel Parke, from the colony of Virginia, in 1708. Parke was an American planter, but turned out a great rascal. In 1736 the negroes, who had now become numerous, led by Klaas, a powerful black, tried to blow up the government house, but the plot was revealed by an Obeah witch. Succeeding years have been marked by hurricanes and pestilences, the year 1835 having been signalized by both of these calamities. There was a previous earthquake in 1833, which gave twenty-three distinct shocks which were felt throughout the islands. The town of St. John's has also been visited by many disastrous fires, the worst of which was in 1841, when the loss reached a million of pounds. In 1825 came the first Anglican bishop, Coleridge, who has written an interesting book upon the Caribbees. St. John's is now the residence of a bishop, and the cathedral, with its two lofty yellow towers, and long nave full of the tombs of English residents, is a striking feature of the town as it is seen from the sea.

The island, though destitute of imposing characteristics, is yet a beautiful member of the group. It is marked by the peculiarities of the tropics. Overhead is the clear blue of the sky. The crystal waters are sparkling in the beams of the blazing sun. Green hills descend to the very shore. Here and there a calm and silent glen opens to the sight. Numerous creeks run far inland, and appear amid the surrounding verdure like chains of silver. A few negro huts are seen nestling at intervals among clumps of trees. At Grace Bay the land looks sprinkled with gold from the flowers of the aloe which grows there in profusion.

In the midst of such natural beauties the higher classes of the inhabitants of these islands while away the hours of daylight until the sun reaches the west and throws his rich beams on every cloud which

> "Throngs to pavilion upon him."

Suddenly he appears to touch the bosom of the flaming waves, and then, sending forth one vivid line of glory, he sinks to rest upon his golden couch. I wish that I could write with truth as well as poetry,

> "Now comes still evening on;"

but no sooner does the sun go down, than sounds of all sorts fill the air. Negro men and women and children gather in groups and begin to gabble, crickets and frogs raise their shrill pipes, mosquitoes hum, and cockroaches scrape the floors or crawl in myriads over the tables, while in country places land crabs clatter about, owls hoot, and multitudes of insects make unmusical noises. We were fortunate in sleeping upon a steamer most of our nights, and, being anchored some distance from shore, enjoyed a peace which the landsman could not secure.

In advance of our arrival we had sent word to have a turtle dinner prepared, and as this delicacy is to be had in great quantity, visions of rich green fat, and white meat, and yellow eggs, filled the imaginations of the epicureans of the party. But such dreams were destined to a rude awaking. Our restaurateur was overwhelmed by the size of the order which he received, and no one who dined that day at Antigua desired to repeat the experience, even for the fun of seeing a mob of negro men and women scramble after dinner in the street for bits of silver which were lavishly scattered among them like corn among a flock of chickens. The stately turtle soup of the lord-mayor of London, which I have eaten on several occasions, is more to my taste, even though it be suspected of relationship to a calf's head, than all the real turtle cooked in this far-off West Indian island.

When we had eaten the banquet and seen the sights, we bade farewell to the town of St. John's, its streets of white wooden houses with green blinds, its grand cathedral and miniature harbor, and sailed due south towards a mighty mass of dark green land, over which clouds were continually rolling and tossing, half revealing, half concealing the peaks and ridges of what we soon learned to know as Guadeloupe, one of the largest and strangest of the islands of the archipelago.

XI

WITCHCRAFT AND SUPERSTITION

IGNORANCE AND CREDULITY OF THE NEGROES — OBEAH, WHAT IT IS AND HOW PRACTISED — SIMILAR BELIEFS IN OTHER NATIONS — ANANSI, JUMBEE AND DUPPY STORIES — SPIRITUALISM AND HYPNOTISM

No account of a tour in the Caribbees would be complete without reference to the superstitions of the negroes. One cannot talk with them, or visit their cabins, or observe their habits, without recognizing the fact that they are like children in their belief in ghosts and devils and evil influences. These have led them to frightful practices in the past, and I was credibly informed, that while there is apparent advance in knowledge and civilization, there are places in the islands where dense superstition and barbarous customs still prevail. Among these superstitions none has been more potent than the "Obeah," concerning which I shall give some facts, derived chiefly from persons who from residence in the West Indies and familiar acquaintance with the negroes, have had abundant opportunities of observa-

A WEST INDIAN TYPE

tion. Among the writers who have treated the subject Père Labat has been most frequently referred to, but more than two centuries have passed since his interesting work was published. It is still an important aid to the tourist among the Caribbees, so far as general topography, natural history, and phenomena are concerned. But the state of society, and the manners and customs of the people, are much changed from what they were in his days. Carmichael's "Domestic Manners of the People of the West Indies"; "West Indian Folk-lore," by Mary P. Milne; Hesketh J. Bell's book upon "Obeah," as well as the books of Mr. F. H. Ober, to whom I have more than once referred, contain chapters upon these subjects, and I have availed myself of all of them.

The term "Obeah" is most probably derived from "Obi," a word used on the east coast of Africa to denote witchcraft, sorcery, and fetichism in general. The etymology of Obi has been traced to a very antique source, stretching far back into Egyptian mythology. A serpent in the Egyptian language was called "Ob" or "Aub." "Obion" is still the Egyptian name for a serpent. Moses, in the name of God, forbade the Israelites even to inquire of the demon "Ob," which is translated in our Bible, charmer or wizard, divinator or sorcerer. The witch of Endor is called "Oub" or "Ob," translated Pythonissa, and "Oubois" was the name of the basilisk, or royal serpent, emblem of the sun and an ancient oracular deity of Egypt.

Hesketh Bell, writing from St. Vincent, says that "the Obeah of the negro is nothing more nor less than a belief in witchcraft, and this operates upon them to such a degree as not unfrequently to produce death. There are few Indian estates upon which there is not one or more Obeah men or women; the negroes know who they are, but it is difficult for white people to find them out. The way they proceed is this: A negro takes a dislike to a negro or negroes, either upon the same estate with himself or upon another; he goes to the Obeah woman and tells her that he will give money or something else as payment if she will Obeah such and such persons. The Obeah woman then goes to those people, and tells them she has Obeahed them. Slow poison is at times secretly administered, but in by far the greater number of cases the mind only is affected; the imagination becomes more and more alarmed, the spirits sink, lassitude and loss of appetite ensue, and death ends the drama.

"The practice of Obeah is too common among the negroes, and very fatal to them. I know of an instance where fifteen people, in the course of a few months, died of no other cause. It is vain to reason with them. 'Missis, I'm Obeahed, I know I'll go dead,' is all you can obtain from them. Negroes so firmly believe this that they have bottles hung round and about their houses, and in their grounds, full of some sort of infusion which they prepare to prevent the Obeah from affecting them; they often wear an armlet, or some such thing, for the same purpose.

"The practice of Obeah is death by the laws of St. Vincent, but there is no possibility of conviction. Negroes believe that spirits occasionally appear, and that devils, or, as they call them, 'Jumbees,' are frequently to be seen; nay, that Jumbee sometimes compels them to go away with him; but I rather think they make a convenience of Jumbee upon such occasions. The name is different, but the truth is negroes believe in witchcraft; and so do many of the lower orders in Britain. I have seen country servants in the county of Mid Lothian who were as firm believers in it as any negro can be. I have seen a dairymaid churn with the dairy locked for fear of a man coming in whose eye she declared would spoil the butter. I have often reasoned with this woman, who was in other respects a shrewd, sensible female for her station in life, and she never ceased to tell me that if I disbelieved in witches I must disbelieve the Bible; there was no arguing with her, for in her opinion it was sacred ground. I have also often heard the lower classes in Scotland use the same argument. Not long ago a respectable man in one of the western counties of England sent to borrow a churn from a lady of my acquaintance, because, as he alleged, 'the devil had got into his churn and he could not make butter in it.'"

Half a century since, the practice of Obeah caused so much loss of slave property by poisoning that it was found necessary to enact the most stringent laws for its repression, and an ordinance was passed in all the West Indian colonies, imposing heavy penalties on any person found guilty of dealing in Obeah. Unfortunately, through the knowledge possessed by some of the old negroes of numerous bushes and plants, unknown to medicine, but found in every tropical wood, it is to be feared that many deaths might still be traced to the agency of these Obeah men. The secret and insidious manner in which this crime is generally perpetrated makes detection exceedingly difficult. A Roman Catholic priest, who was asked to give his opinion upon the subject, replied: "Ah, my dear sir, I can't remember half I hear and notice on these ever-present superstitions of the people, but I assure you that it is one of the greatest obstacles I meet with in my work among my parishioners; these foolish but so deeply rooted beliefs of theirs in the power of Obeah and witchcraft meet me at every turn, and after talking hours and trying to prove to them how ridiculous and senseless all these ideas are, I only obtain a seeming acquiescence and make no lasting impression. I have tried everything to combat the baneful influence, and endeavored to make them ashamed of their ignorance and credulity, but with precious little effect. I have even adopted the Japanese custom of punishing a whole street for the misdeeds of one criminal living in it, by refusing the sacraments for a time to a whole family, if a member of it be known to be dabbling in Obeah all to the same purpose."

"West Indian Folk-lore" contains many similar instances of the influence of Obeah upon the negroes. It has also a collection of fairy tales and silly stories with which the people amused each other, from which I extract an example: "In the West Indies if you desire to be told a fairy tale or anything of the kind you must ask for 'Anansi' stories. In the old days these were usually told at local gatherings of the people; such as weddings or funerals, the latter being equal occasions for festivity with the former. The old women keep the children quiet with these tales, and the small, white 'buccra,' sitting by its nurse, will have a flood of folk-lore wasted on its entertainment, which an elder interested in the same will vainly endeavor to hear, the narrator repeating: 'Dat foolishness; wonder missus car to har dat.' Anansi stories, which are those usually told to children, owe their name to a mysterious personage who plays the principal part in them — a hairy, old man with long nails, very ugly, called brother or Father Anansi. In some way Anansi bears a resemblance to the Scandinavian 'Troll' or 'Scrattle,' and the 'Lubber fiend' of the English north country; and his character is not unlike that of the German 'Reinecke Fuchs,' or the Japanese 'Kitsuri Fox,' thievish and cunning. Here is one of the Anansi stories: Anansi and Baboon were disputing one day which was fattest; Anansi said he was sure he was fat, but Baboon declared he was fatter. Then Anansi proposed they should prove it; so they made a fire and agreed that they should hang up before it and see which would drop most fat. Baboon hung up Anansi first, but no fat dropped. Then Anansi hung up Baboon, and very soon the fat began to drop, which smelt so good that Anansi cut a slice of Baboon and said: 'O brother Baboon, you fat for true.' But Baboon didn't speak. So Anansi said: 'Well, speak or not speak, I'll eat you every bit to-day,' which he really did. But when he had eaten up all Baboon, the bits joined together in his stomach, and began to pull him about so much that he was obliged to go to a doctor. The doctor told him not to eat anything for some days, then he was to get a ripe banana and hold it to his mouth. When Baboon, who would be hungry, smelt the banana, he would be sure to run up to eat it, and so he would run out of his mouth. So Anansi starved himself and got the banana, and did as the doctor told him, but when he put the banana to his mouth he was so hungry he couldn't help eating it. So he didn't get rid of Baboon, which went on pulling him, until he went back to the doctor, who took a banana and held it to Anansi's mouth, and very soon the baboon jumped up to catch it, and ran out of his mouth, and Anansi was glad to get rid of him. And baboons to this very day like bananas. Besides Anansi stories there are also Duppy or Jumbee stories which relate solely to ghosts, and resemble what the French call 'revenants,' the Germans 'wald gheist,' and are also similar to the Irish 'fetch.'"

The want of grace and description about the folk-tales seems to be less striking wherever the Frenchman or Spaniard has had dominion; in Martinique, for instance, there seems to be more romance and graceful sentiment about the negro and Creole superstitions than in the English islands, the ghost stories are more weird and powerful, and the expressions used are happier and more refined. Perhaps the grace and *esprit* of the old French settlers have left an impression upon their descendants.

In Martinique prevails a curious superstition, that of the "diablesse," a beautiful negress with piercing eyes, who passes silently through some lonely cane-piece where men and women are at work, and whatever man she smiles upon must arise sooner or later and follow her — to death, since he is never seen again. This superstition is apparently akin to that prevailing among the Russian peasants, of the Baba Yagas, or witch woman, whose look wiles a man away to death.

People who are out of doors very early in the morning in tropical latitudes, often feel in the midst of the cool freshness, sudden breaths of hot air — a curious phenomenon. This gives rise to another superstition, and the negroes say they are passing by "Jumbee's fireplace," where he made his fire over night. The beautiful silk cotton tree is supposed to be Jumbee's favorite haunt, and a negro is loth to cut down one of these trees, certain that some evil will overtake him after so doing. For this a lover of nature is inclined to bless Jumbee, as the means of saving many of those grand kings of the forest.

The advance of education will doubtless do much to dispel these silly and dangerous superstitions, but when we realize how many people are under the control of spiritualists, and Christian scientists, and faith cures, in the most enlightened and Christian communities, it does not seem strange that races that have only been emancipated from bondage for a few generations, and from heathenism for perhaps a few centuries, should be thus blinded and deluded.

XII

GUADELOUPE

UP SALT RIVER — HURRICANE WORK — A GREAT STEAM-
ING VOLCANO — COFFEE PLANTATIONS AND CULTURE
— BRILLIANT MARKET SCENE — EXTRACTS FROM PÈRE
LABAT

It was evening when we saw the gleam of the lighthouse at Point à Pitre on Guadeloupe, and let go the anchor in the harbor. The electric lights still shone in the town and one or two boats came out to the steamer, but even the quartette of young men, who were usually ready for an excursion ashore at any hour of the day or evening, were content to wait till morning. Some of the party were polishing up their French in the cabin; for Guadeloupe and Martinique inhabitants speak only the French language, though their speech is not the dialect which Americans call "Parisian." The negroes throughout the islands speak a French patois which is hardly intelligible to other people, and is a meaningless jargon to foreigners. Morning revealed to us a beautiful landlocked bay with a thoroughly tropical aspect. Mangroves lined the banks of the river, cocoanut and other palms overhung the town and grew in groves beyond its limits, tall breadfruit trees with rounded tops and dark foliage diversified the landscape, and a nearer view revealed orange orchards, and gardens full of hibiscus, begonias, and roses. Upon the right was an immense group of sugar factories, the Usines Centrales, where the sugar-canes are brought by the planters and sold to be manufactured into sugar. Huge smokestacks were vomiting out black smoke, and the industry was in full blast, as we landed at a stone pier from a little naphtha launch which plies in the harbor.

The town of Point à Pitre lies on the southwestern side of the island, at the southern mouth of a river called Salee, or Salt River. It has an excellent harbor protected on every side. The town is new, having been rebuilt not many years ago, after a fire which laid the old town in ashes. It had previously been shaken down by an earthquake, and blown to pieces by a hurricane. The first town was built of stone, which the earthquake tumbled into ruins; the second was built of wood to prevent damage from this source, but a hurricane blew the frail structures away; and fire burned up the next town. The present town is laid out upon broad, straight streets, with several public squares, and many fine buildings. It is said to be built of iron-framed houses filled in with brick, to guard against the varied attacks from the elements which have proved so destructive in the past.

Guadeloupe, of which island Point à Pitre is one of the chief towns, is the largest of the West India Islands which belong to France, and has an important commerce. It lies in latitude fifteen degrees north, and longitude sixty-one degrees west, embraces with its outlying islands six hundred and twenty-five square miles, and has a population of more than one hundred and fifty thousand souls, three-quarters of whom are blacks. The main island is divided by Salt River, which is navigable for small boats, but is largely swamp. Guadeloupe proper lies on the west and Grande Terre on the east of the river, and each division is about thirty-five miles long; though Guadeloupe is a third wider than Grande Terre, being eighteen miles across from sea to sea, and contains the mountain range, whose summit is the steaming volcano, Soufrière. Grande Terre is low, flat, and marshy and is not composed of lava but of coral and marine shells; Basse Terre is a vast mass of volcanic débris rising five thousand feet into the air, clothed with majestic primeval forests whose trees are of enormous proportions. We came to the southern end of the island upon our return trip and did not land, but we lay to for an hour to take the mail, and consequently could reconnoitre through the field-glass. This view revealed deep ravines whose sides were covered with dense forests out of which towered groves of vast magnitude, and now and then as the cloud-caps lifted, we caught sight of the awful blackness of the Soufrière, the crater formed of a dozen peaks like giant teeth of the jaws of hell. Steam and sulphurous smoke poured forth from the abyss, and it was a relief when the pearly vapors once more shrouded the horrid place from mortal view. This is no imaginary picture of a volcano. In 1797 the Soufrière hurled forth dense masses of ashes and pumice and sulphur smoke; in 1843 its convulsions shook the island and tumbled its towns into ruins; and before and since that date, smoke by day and flames by night have shown its fiery temper and unquenched power for evil, yet the French people increase, prosper, and are merry here.

There are numerous coffee plantations on Guadeloupe, and also on Dominica. At the latter island I met a young Englishman, who had a small coffee plantation, which gave him a comfortable support and a visit home once in five years. The coffee plants are usually raised from seeds sown in beds, upon the mountains, where the thermometer varies from fifty-five degrees Fahrenheit in winter, to eighty degrees in the heat of summer. When they are two years old, the small shoots are set out in rows six feet apart each way. In three years they begin to yield; they are increasingly fruitful for fifteen or twenty years, and live for a century. It was February when we were at Guadeloupe, and the trees were in bloom; the fruit ripens from August to December, but blooms and green fruit and the ripened berry may be sometimes seen at once during the latter part of the year. The berry is red, of the size and color of a cherry, and coffee is made from the kernel or seed, which is divided into two hemispheres. This seed goes through a variety of processes before it becomes the coffee of commerce, and is prepared for use in the delicious beverage which is known all over the world. Most of the coffee of the French islands goes naturally to France, but it is not as cheap as the South American product, and its cultivation is encouraged by government bounties. The coffee and sugar interests do not conflict, for the former occupies the highland and the latter the lowland.

The government of this French island is vested in a governor and his council, and a general council of thirty members. Basse Terre is the capital, and the jurisdiction embraces the islands Guadeloupe, Marie Galante, Désirade, Les Saintes, and St. Martin.

Columbus discovered these islands in 1493 — naming the second one after one of his ships. France took possession of them in 1635, and after many changes of owners, in 1816 they became her permanent possession, and her policy has made them prosperous and productive, in spite of earthquakes and hurricanes. Slavery, which had been abolished in the English islands in 1834, continued in Guadeloupe till 1848.

Landing at Point à Pitre from the naphtha launch at a pier near the fish market, our company dispersed through the town, some seeking the sugar mills, and others the market and museum. The market is held in a covered building in one of the principal squares, and presented a novel and exciting scene. Several hundred women — black, yellow, quadroon, and octoroon, with very little negro blood and hardly any negro features — were chattering and chaffering, screaming and gesticulating like monkeys, over little piles of fruit and vegetables and roots and meats and bouquets of flowers. They wore loose and long flowing gowns of gaudy and brilliant prints, which they held half-way up to their waists as they walked in the market-place. On their heads were turbans which equalled anything in Damascus or Assouan, formed of Madras handkerchiefs, rolled and twisted about the head in many folds with one end sticking up at the top. All the women wore jewels, necklaces of huge beads, great hoops and cylinders of gold in their ears, bracelets and rings without number. The passion of the Frenchwoman and of the blacks for the display of jewelry and gay clothing seems to have united in this race of islanders, and their appearance was gay and festive in the extreme.

The women of Guadeloupe are good-looking, and we saw a few Creole girls who were beautiful. They had pure and fine complexions, brown and pale with a rose tint on the cheeks, and a thin skin through which the blue veins in the forehead could be traced. Their hair fell in glossy ringlets; dark and lustrous eyes half hid by long drooping eyelashes, and pencilled brows, relieved the prevailing color of the face. Pearly teeth gleamed through thin coral lips, and when pleased or excited the whole face seemed to shine as water gleams in the sunlight. They were petite as compared with the large-limbed and broad-shouldered black women, with small and beautifully shaped hands and feet, and forms which might have posed for a Venus de Medici. Their voices were not soft and pleasant like those of the negroes, but treble and high-pitched, so that the illusion produced by their beauty was often dispelled as soon as they spoke.

MILK SELLER--GUADELOUPE

The population of Guadeloupe seemed to be industrious, thrifty, and happy. The women came into town bearing on their heads baskets filled with bottles of milk, fruits and vegetables, coffee and vanilla beans. The shops were numerous and well supplied, and an air of activity and prosperity pervaded the place. There was none of the solicitation and begging among the street negroes of Guadeloupe which is so great a nuisance in most of these West Indian towns. "Father, I beg you a penny," said many a man and woman and boy to me from St. Kitt's to Barbados. I have not been begged more persistently in Italy and Spain than under the English flag in these islands. Travellers generally have themselves to blame for encouraging this kind of tax, but the negroes are such cheerful and natural mendicants that it is almost impossible to refuse them, especially when their rags and nakedness offer *prima facie* evidence of destitution, but these evidences were lacking at Point à Pitre.

There is an interesting museum in the town which contains specimens of the animals, birds, and reptiles of the islands, and also many curiosities and remains of the Carib tribes who dwelt here when Columbus came. There were some living specimens of the mongoose. This rodent kills snakes, especially the dreaded fer-de-lance (whose bite is instant death);

there were also some specimens in alcohol of this deadly snake. We never saw one alive in all our tours, though our ears were filled with stories about them, and we had read the thrilling descriptions of Père Labat till it seemed as if the Windward Islands without the fer-de-lance would be very tame places to travel in. A few extracts translated from Père Labat's chapters on Guadeloupe will be read with interest in this connection. Writing of the sulphur waters, he says: —

"There is a part of Anse, particularly near the river, where the beach is covered with rocks and pebbles of different sizes, but the rest is white, firm sand, which makes an agreeable walk. About three hundred paces to the left of the church I noticed that the waters of the sea in some places were bubbling. I went out in a little canoe to see if it was really true, as they told me, that one could cook eggs and fish in the water. At a distance of about three fathoms from the shore, where the water was four feet deep, I found it so warm in these bubbling places that I could not hold my hand in it. I sent for eggs and boiled them by holding them suspended in the water by means of my handkerchief. On the beach I found the surface of the sand was no hotter opposite the places where the water boiled than anywhere else, but digging with my hand for five or six inches I began to feel heat, and at a depth of two feet I found the sand burning hot and smoking with a strong odor of sulphur.

"They took me to a sort of pond or pool, where the water was whitish, as if it had been disturbed. Spouts of water were constantly seen, more frequently in the centre of the pool. I took some of this water in a shell and it was really boiling. When it cooled I tasted it, and found it good, but with a slight taste of sulphur. . . . It is a pity that these waters are not in the hands of people who could make use of them, for it is certain that they are excellent for many diseases. I was assured that many hydropathics had been completely cured after having sweated in this sand, and many others with chills and nervous affections found relief."

Respecting one of the most famous birds of these islands, he writes: "We were at Guadeloupe at the season for hunting certain birds called 'devils.' They were to be found in Guadeloupe and Dominique, where they came at certain times of the year to lay their eggs and hatch them. This bird is about the size of a grown chicken, its plumage is black, and its wings are long and strong; its legs are short with feet like a duck's, but with long claws; its beak is long and hooked and very hard; it has large eyes which serve it well in the night, but are so useless in the day that it cannot stand the light or distinguish objects, and if surprised by daylight far from its nest, the poor bird dashes itself against all obstacles in its path and finally falls to the earth. The manner of hunting devils is to force them out of their holes into the sunlight by means of dogs, when they are easily caught and their necks wrung." Again, speaking of the production of ginger, one of the most profitable exports, he says: "Ginger comes from the root of a plant about two feet high. This plant needs good but light earth to grow in, which is the reason it thrives in the soil of the Grande Terre of Guadeloupe, which is of this quality. They plant the ginger at the end of the rainy season, that is, in October and November, and when it is ripe its leaves become yellow and dry. The plant is then taken up, separated from its roots, and dried by being exposed to the air or wind, but never to the sun, which would consume its delicate substance almost immediately. Thus prepared, ginger will last as long as one wishes to keep it, but of course it is better when fresh."

Guadeloupe left pleasing impressions. It seemed less savage and rude and more interesting than any of the islands we had yet seen. After we had visited the cathedral, the various quarters of the town, the shops and the photographer's and the museum, we entered the launch and were soon on board and steaming on a fine afternoon towards Dominica.

XIII

SABBATH DAY ISLAND

RAINBOWS AMONG THE GROO-GROO PALMS — MONSIEUR COCKROACH AND HIS MAN ISAAC — A RARE MOUNTAIN RIDE — TROPICAL AIRS, SIGHTS AND SOUNDS — A NEW PARADISE WITH SOME SNAKES — HISTORY OF DOMINICA

As we moved along over a waveless sea towards the next landing-place, I remarked especially a phenomenon which had been noticed several times upon the voyage. The island of Guadeloupe, which is one of the largest islands, seemed very small, and appeared to hang as it were between sea and sky. Other travellers have alluded to this appearance which has some of the elements of the mirage, but so far as I have read, no one except Charles Kingsley has attempted an explanation. He ascribes this foreshortening to a combination of causes, among which the extreme clearness of the air, the simplicity of the form of the islands, and their isolation, which prevents comparison with other objects, are chief. Whether the explanation be correct or not, his observation accords with my own when he says that "one fancies at moments that the island does not rise out of the sea, but floats upon it, that it is held in its place not by the roots of the mountains, and deep miles of lava wall below, but by the cloud which has caught it by the top, and will not let it go. Let that cloud but rise and vanish, and the whole beautiful thing will be cast adrift; ready to fetch away before the wind, and (as it will seem often enough to do when viewed through a cabin-port) to slide silently past you while you are sliding past it."

One of the pleasantest afternoons that I remember was the one on which our vessel skirted the leeward side of the bold and beautiful island of Dominica, whose steep shores were bordered with groo-groo palms, and whose lofty heights were clothed in every shade of green, or rather in hues ranging from pale yellow to a sapphire blue; down whose far-reaching valleys waterfalls poured a white line of foam, and on whose lofty spurs and peaks a dozen rainbows were forming and fading, and reforming as the showers shifted with the changing gusts of air. What we saw in outline then was revealed in all its wealth of beauty the next day when we rode on horseback more than half-way across the island, ascending through the valleys and along the mountain side to the height of more than three thousand feet.

We cast anchor in front of the pretty town of Roseau, at the southern end of the island, at six o'clock, and five minutes later the sun went down with a bang from the gun in the fort, and in two minutes more it began to be dark. With the darkness came on board the steamer Monsieur "Cockroach," who is the tourist agent of Dominica. He gathers the horses and guides and attendants for travellers who wish to go to the boiling spring or the lake of the clouds, or to climb to the high places of the Caribbean earth. He notifies "Isaac" and his Creole wife to provide ices, and liquid refreshment, and fruits and a variety of mementos for an approaching company, and he intimates that original Caribs may be seen and heard at the half-way house. How he came by his name I do not know. It does not suggest the man, for he never crawls, and he is clothed in clean white linen, with an immaculate hat. With him we made arrangements for our ride of thirty miles next day, and had no occasion to regret our contract.

The morning was clear and warm. For a wonder in Dominica no rain fell all day in the part of the island which we traversed. At nine o'clock we went ashore and found "Cockroach" waiting for us with about forty horses of various sizes, shapes, and breeds, though the majority of them were tough little ponies evidently accustomed to hard usage and to mountain roads. Captain Fraser and a friend from Quebec were soon off with one company to visit the sulphur springs. Our good Pennsylvania priest and other friends were mounted by the Roman Catholic bishop of Roseau, and they took the course to a lime plantation, returning in the evening with glowing accounts of shady bowers and cooling drinks, and the music of waterfalls and genuine West Indian hospitality. The colonel had a good mount and rode as became a graduate from West Point and a cavalry officer throughout our civil war. The Lawrence quartette were all on hand, but as there are no wheeled vehicles on the island, only one lady accompanied the party.

The young men were in full force with their enthusiastic and never-wearied leader, and this island has rarely had a more intelligent and interested band of visitors. The party followed the valley for a mile or two, wondering at the breadth of the river channel, which was more than fifty feet. A small stream of water ran through the centre, but we were assured that when the rainy season comes a full tide of rushing water fills the course from bank to bank. We soon struck into a woodland road, and realized what it was to be in the midst of tropical vegetation. Great masses of foliage covered the most precipitous and jagged mountains. Looked at from a distance, it seemed as if the mountains were wrapped in vast robes of sheeny silk and velvet, gemmed with rubies, and emeralds, and topazes. Whole expanses of gray-green, shining leaves reflected the sun with dazzling effect. Beyond rose a ridge crowned with palmistes, their tall, smooth stems standing up against the horizon, crowned with an umbrella-shaped top, which waved perceptibly in the wind, even at such an altitude. Near at hand, along the road, which later became only a path, trees and vines were dense and often interlaced. There were breadfruit, mango, lime, and lemon trees; forests of cocoa trees loaded with fruit about the size of a large cucumber, colored according to the stage of development, green, yellow, or rich purple, and seeming to grow directly from the branch without any stem; clumps of green and graceful bamboos rising a hundred feet into the air and waving their feathery tops; huge ceiba trees covered with parasites and orchids; almond trees and giant flamboyants with red blossoms. Further up, in vales and hollows, we came to manifold tree ferns, whose slender stalks supported at the height of twenty or thirty feet the most delicate green lace

INDIGO MAKING—DOMINICA

work parasols and umbrellas that were ever seen. The ravines were full of those of larger growth, and the banks along our path were covered with little ones all infinitely beautiful. Here, too, were banana and tamarind trees loaded with clusters of fruit, while half hid from view by their enormous fronds, some curious red flowers, shaped like lobster's claws, clung to the green stems of a strange plant. I counted fifty kinds of flowers on a single bank, and the ferns and mosses were innumerable.

As we rose higher, the air, which had been warm and languorous, became fresh and clear, and the ocean could now and then be seen on each side of the island. Anon we descended into deep valleys, where limes were cultivated on a plantation, and into denser valleys, where nothing met the eye but an ocean of foliage, heights crowned with trees and interlaced with shrubs, a Colorado cañon resplendent with rich vegetation of the rarest and most beautiful sorts. However high we climbed, there were higher mountains, and the more we explored, the greater the wonders and the rarer the treasures were. Language utterly fails to describe the richness and beauty and variety of trees and shrubs and flowers and greens and colors in nature, which ravished our eyes. Odors, delicious and sensuous, filled the air, and the place seemed in all respects a woodland paradise. The strange songs of birds which we did not know often startled us. Beautiful humming-birds of peacock-colored plumage, or black, with garnet spotted throats, or golden green, glistening like winged jewels in the sunshine, flew about, and not hovering on the wing as they do in our gardens, but lighting on twigs and plants, they gazed upon us with more curiosity than fear.

Through such beauties we rode on and on for a dozen miles to a lovely fresh-water lake embosomed in the hills and girt about with tropical forests; after resting here and comparing our gathered treasures of plants and fruits and flowers, the party retraced its steps to the half-way house, where Isaac, in obedience to "Cockroach," had provided a good luncheon. After luncheon we were entertained with Creole songs and dances, which have evidently descended from the days when planters lived on these islands with their families of slaves. The melodies were sweet and quaint, unlike modern negro songs, and yet with little resemblance to the music of civilization. The dances were graceful and pleasing, and consisted largely of swaying motions of the body and gestures of the arms and head to rhythmic music. These pleasures ended, we rode down the mountain and through the little town, full of delightful memories of lovely scenes.

Roseau, the chief town upon the island of Dominica, is picturesquely situated on the sea at the mouth of a river which comes rushing and roaring down through hills which, though broken and ragged, are yet densely covered with a vast variety of foliage. It is a little place, with a few streets running at right angles, paved with large stones, and ending in three roads which lead into the mountains and up and down the coast. There is a row of solid houses near the landing. The other houses are small and mostly built of wood, one story high and twenty feet square. Some are even smaller. I went into a little enclosure containing a one-story house, a cocoanut tree and a breadfruit tree, and also a small garden patch. A man and two women were squatting around a kettle containing the dinner. The door of the house stood open, and its one room was only large enough for an ordinary-sized bed and a chair beside it. There were hooks on the rough board walls, and clothes and tin dishes hung indiscriminately upon them. This was the home of five people, three adults and two children. The climate is warm and they live mostly out of doors. But as there is much rain in Dominica these people must be wet a great part of the time. I passed a Sunday here, and attended the Wesleyan Methodist and English churches. The latter is a large stone building with a clock, and some grand palmistes in front of it. The old French Catholic Cathedral is larger than both the other churches, as it well may be, for almost the entire population is of that faith. Opposite the English church is the governor's house and a well-stocked botanical garden. Each of the islands has a garden of this sort, well kept and a source of evident pleasure and pride to the inhabitants. Each town of any size has also a public library with a fair assortment of books, and a reading room. I remembered that New York has as yet no public library, and that the charter for a botanical garden has only just now been obtained. The frequent showers and hot sunshine in Dominica cause a prolific growth of vegetation. The gardens are full of trees and plants, flowering vines cover the walls, and there are many birds and butterflies flitting about in the sunshine.

I must add a few interesting facts about Dominica. The island is twenty-nine miles long by sixteen broad, and is the most southern of the islands belonging to what is called by the British the Leeward group. Its area is two hundred and ninety-one miles, its population twenty-seven thousand. The island is noted for the amount of its rainfall, which greatly adds to its fertility. The thermometer stands at eighty degrees Fahrenheit in the shade during the months of June, July, and August; and at seventy degrees during the other months. The sun is vertical from May to August, and the inhabitants *ascii* (or shadowless) at noon. The longest day is thirteen hours, the shortest ten. September and October are the least healthy months of the year. Its exports are cattle, cocoa, lime juice, rum, molasses, and sugar. The chief town is Roseau. It was discovered by Columbus on Sunday, Nov. 3, 1493, hence its name. It was colonized by the French, whom the Caribs allowed to settle. In 1748, by the treaty of Aix-la-Chapelle, England and France stipulated that Dominica should be regarded as neutral, and left to the Caribs. Later, Frenchmen settled on the island, but in 1756 it became by conquest a dependency of Great Britain. Cultivable lands were sold, and yielded to the crown 312,092 pounds sterling. The French settlers were generously treated, and allowed to remain secure in their possessions.

In 1771 Dominica was constituted a separate government. In 1776, attracted by its fertility, the French took advantage of the war between Great Britain and her North American colonies and attacked Dominica from Martinique. The French inhabitants of the islands invited them to do this, and aided by making the English soldiers at the fort drunk and then filling the cannon with sand. The English troops and colonists made desperate resistance, but surrendered in 1778 and were badly treated. In 1783 the island was restored to the British. A final attack was made by the French in 1805 under General La Grange, who landed on Roseau, but the French only held the place for five days, levying contributions and destroying the shipping; then they re-embarked. This was the last invasion, and the inhabitants still date from La Grange or 1805.

XIV

CARIBS OF DOMINICA AND ST. VINCENT

COLUMBUS AND THE CARIBS — A FORGOTTEN LANGUAGE — THE REMNANT OF A PEOPLE — JENNY THE MONKEY AND HER REFLECTIONS

This is perhaps as good a place as any to tell the story of the Carib Indians who once dominated these islands. We saw a few of their descendants, and it is claimed that upon their reservation at Dominica, and at St. Vincent, there are still some families of pure Carib blood. When Mr. Ober visited them in 1876 he found about twenty families. His last visit, in 1892, was made for the purpose of ascertaining how many of these Caribs could be prevailed upon to go to the Chicago Columbian Exposition; it being the intention of the managers to include all the representatives of America in their ethnological department. At that time there were about two hundred Caribs in Dominica, and of this number less than fifteen families were uncontaminated with negro blood. They were living in very much the same style as their ancestors did when Columbus found them in 1493.

Columbus saw the Caribs first, not on this island, but at Carbet, near the point of Capesterre, on the eastern coast of Guadeloupe. They were dwelling in huts covered with palm branches; they made cassava bread from the manihot plant, and caught fish along the shores, using the boats for the purpose which they had dug out of gum tree logs; and they wove baskets like those which are now offered to the traveller.

But when Columbus found them, they were not the peaceful and indolent people who now bear their name. Irving describes them as trained to war from their infancy, able to use the bow and arrow with unerring accuracy, and having sufficient knowledge of the heavenly bodies to enable them to calculate times and seasons. They let their coarse black hair grow long, painted their faces and bodies, and both men and women fought the Spaniards desperately. Proofs were found in their huts that they were cannibals. They were treated as such by the Spaniards, but they struck back, and many a proud hidalgo bit the dust before they were subdued. Columbus called them Caribs or cannibals, both of which names are designations of valor or strength. The Caribs of South America claim a similar meaning for their name, and the author of " Myths of the New World," thinks that Shakespeare drew the plot of " The

Tempest" from South American mythology; that "Caliban," the savage native of the island in the play, is undoubtedly the word "Carib," often spelled among South American Indians "Caribana" and "Calibani."

Another curious fact, is that Robinson Crusoe's "Man Friday" was a Carib, and his "island" was Tobago in the Caribbean Sea, which we saw but did not visit. But they had changed little in a hundred years, as may be seen from the account given by a writer of the last century: "The Caribs are of clear copper color, and have sleek, black hair; their persons are well made, but they disfigure their faces by flattening their foreheads in infancy. They live chiefly by fishing in the rivers and the sea, or by fowling in the woods, and in both pursuits they use their arrows with wonderful dexterity. It is said they will kill the smallest bird with an arrow at a great distance, or transfix a fish at a considerable depth in the sea. They display also great ingenuity in making curiously wrought panniers or baskets of silk grass or the leaves and bark of trees." They have preserved this art of basket making to the present day. I bought at Roseau a beautiful and useful basket, about the size of a small trunk. It is chiefly valuable on account of its lightness and also because it is waterproof. It is made from a plant called mahoe, in two thicknesses, with layers of wild plantain between.

This basket was not cheap, for the materials of which it is made are scarce, and the makers have a monopoly of the market, but it is a most serviceable article at home or in travel. I saw sets or "nests" of these baskets, as well as of another smaller and more delicate sort of Indian basket which is common in the islands.

The Carib reservation in Dominica extends from Mahoe River to Crayfish River, about three miles along the Atlantic coast, and as far as they choose to cultivate inland. They raise the yam, sweet potato, cassava, banana, plantain, and tannier. Their little settlement, a mere hamlet, is called Salibia. Here they live, no longer warlike or enterprising, satisfied with the careless and monotonous existence of uncivilized man. Of the whole number of two hundred, perhaps ten could make a canoe and twenty weave a perfect basket. The majority display no mechanical ingenuity. They raise the vegetables and gather the fruits which grow almost without planting and mature without care.

Their ancient language is no longer used to any extent, and a patois made up of French and English in unequal proportions, is their common, and to a stranger unintelligible tongue. Though called Indians, they have little in common with the tribes which we designate by that general name. Their faces are oval, with broad and handsome foreheads, rather high cheek bones, the eyes far apart, the nose regular and well proportioned, the mouth of moderate size with rather thin lips; their skin is yellow or golden brown, and they have long, abundant, and fine hair, purple-black in color, like the hair of many Spanish women, though not of so fine a quality as theirs. They have graceful forms in youth, and very well shaped arms and legs, with small hands and feet. Like all the people of these islands, they stand erect, hold their heads with natural grace, and walk with an air of dignity and honor. But they grow old soon and are then even more hideous than the negroes about them. They are nominally Roman Catholics and the priest of Roseau visits them and administers the sacraments. Their ancestors believed in some sort of a future state, and in a supreme being to whom they offered sacrifice. The brave among them were supposed to go after death to a state of felicity; the cowardly were banished to dreary deserts and rugged mountains.

Mr. Ober lived for two weeks with the Caribs of St. Vincent, in a little wattled hut thatched with leaves, for the purpose of securing a vocabulary of their ancient language. He found but six families of pure Carib blood and but a few persons who could speak the Carib tongue, and most of these were women. He says that "they have few terms of abuse, and about the most offensive is, 'you are no good,' or 'you are no livelier than a turtle.' They have no word for virtue, which even at the present day is rare indeed. In counting they cannot express themselves above twenty and then only by means of the fingers and toes. My wife is 'my heart'; a boy is 'a little man'; the fingers are the 'babes of the hands'; the rainbow is 'God's plume.' There is a people among them called 'Black Caribs,' formed by the union of the American and the Ethiopian. These comprise a small community on the northwestern shore of St. Vincent, at a place called Morne Ronde." Throughout the island he found traces of the ancient inhabitants, weapons, domestic utensils, axes, spearheads, chisels, and fragments of pottery. Some of the rocks are covered with rude hieroglyphics, but there is no reason to believe that the Caribs ever came to or from the continent of North America. If they came originally from the southern continent, as is likely, they had no relation to the Aztecs, but were a ruder and more warlike people.

Some of the South American Caribs were passengers with us on the homeward voyage under the care of an agent of Barnum's show. He was bringing them to New York to join the ethnological department of the great show, which was about to make its annual progress through the United States. They were good-looking, yellow, long-haired, red painted men and women, stout-bodied and with extremely broad shoulders and strong limbs. The children were fat, with white teeth and mischievous black eyes, but they were not half so amusing as "Jenny," the monkey which one of our party bought at St. Kitt's. She was a veritable actress and was often brought out for our amusement. A more pathetic and ludicrous scene was never enacted, than that which took place when she first saw her own reflection in a mirror. No Carib Indian child or adult could give so interesting a performance. But alas, these Caribs are immortals, though their day on earth is nearly done.

It was sad to meditate upon the speedy extinction of such a race. Once they were brave, powerful, and in happy possession of some of the fairest regions of the earth. Now, the few remnants are spiritless and degraded, without even a knowledge of their ancestors, unable to speak their language, content with a mere existence, and gradually yielding to the pressure of a civilization which is sweeping them into oblivion.

XV

ISLE DE MARTINIQUE

FRANCE IN THE TROPICS — FOUNTAINS AND FLOWING WATERS — MARDI GRAS AND WILD REVELRIES — THE "SWIZZLE" AND ITS USES — SNAKE STORIES — EMPRESS JOSEPHINE, HER EARLY LIFE HERE AND HER STATUE — MADAME DE MAINTENON

WE had been looking forward to Martinique as the queen of the Caribbees, and in some respects were not disappointed. The island is one of the most beautiful in its outlines, admirably cultivated, peopled with lively and enterprising inhabitants, and full of sights and sounds which attract and entertain the traveller. Its lofty Montagne Pelée is hooded with clouds a great part of the time, but now and then the summit is revealed, a mass of green, sky-piercing and grand, supported by vast flanks that sweep in graceful undulations to the sea. There are luxuriant plantations, dense and dark forests, villages upon the high slopes, and two picturesque towns, St. Pierre and Fort de France, along the shores. The anchor of the *Madiana* dropped into the azure sea, and straightway a little fleet of coffin-shaped boxes, propelled by naked boys each with two little paddles, came hurrying out to meet us. They had come as at St. Thomas to dive for coins, and soon they were plunging into the harbor after little silver pieces which the passengers lavishly threw overboard. The boys were quick to see the coins as they touched the water, and tumbled out of their queer tubs in a wild scramble for them. Long before the coin was out of sight, they had swam beneath it, and with the speed of fishes reappeared, holding the treasure high uplifted in their hands. This scene was repeated daily and at all hours, and the lithe brown bodies of these coin fishers became familiar objects about the vessel while we lay in the harbor of St. Pierre.

The town is unique, a strange mingling of France and the tropics. It lies along the curve of a pretty bay and rises in terraces upon the mountain side. The prevailing color of the stone houses is a golden yellow, which is set off by red tiled roofs here and there. A hurricane desolated the place a few years since, and when the houses were rebuilt many of them were roofed with corrugated iron, which has none of the picturesque effects of the old red tiles. The houses of the town are mostly built along narrow streets, and have unglazed windows, which at night are covered with heavy wooden shutters, in which there are movable slats. The streets are steep and well paved, and through the wide gutters a constant stream of water pours down, carrying all the sewage to the sea. This rushing mountain water is the feature of the town; it rises in numerous pretty fountains and is the public scavenger of the island. Men with huge poles and hooks keep the gutters from becoming clogged and clear the cesspools at the foot of the streets, which otherwise would become stuffed with cocoanut shells and palm leaves and plantain skins, and all sorts of rubbish which are constantly thrown into these street channels. On the quay are thousands of hogsheads of molasses, and casks of rum and bags of sugar, waiting shipment; powerful blacks swarm among them, rolling and carrying them from place to place.

There was not much work performed after our first day in Martinique, for it was the festival of Mardi Gras and the people gave themselves up to a strange mingling of devotion and dissipation. The costumes of the women are fantastic and bewildering at any time, but as the festival advanced, they became as grotesque and brilliant as any scene that was ever set upon the stage. The various faces of black, and red, and brown, and yellow, and of delicate cream and rouge, were a study for a painter or an ethnol-

ST. PIERRE—MARTINIQUE

ogist, and the straight bodies and easy swinging gait of the unshod feet of most of the inhabitants produced a novel impression upon the beholder. On Sunday morning high mass was celebrated in the Cathedral and afterwards the whole town seemed to be given up to revelry and dissipation. Bands of masked men and women paraded the streets dressed in the most vulgar style. As night came on the tumult increased, the great theatre was crowded to suffocation, and yelling, laughing, dancing, and deviltry of all sorts made night hideous. We were glad of the refuge which the steamer afforded from such a pandemonium, but even at our anchorage we could hear the blare of the trumpets and the shouts of the excited crowds upon the shore. I had seen the festival in New Orleans and elsewhere, where great license was allowed, but here it became, before it was ended, a wild and disgusting orgy.

The island contrasts favorably with those which belong to Great Britain. There is none of that abject poverty and incessant beggary on the French islands which meet one at every turn in the English possessions. The people have an air of thrift and self-respect which finds expression in the cleanliness, dress, and taste displayed in their streets, houses, and costumes. Some of the women are very pretty and they wear their gay dresses in a style which leaves one arm and shoulder bare, and with their long skirts looped up at the hips. A large proportion of the population are of mixed blood, and have the fondness for ornaments and display which is common to all half-breeds. At the Cathedral, a large and handsome building with a sweet chime of bells, I saw a congregation which filled the place, and was composed, like most Roman Catholic assemblies, chiefly of women. Nearly all of these wore yellow and green turbans, made of Madras handkerchiefs with one end sticking out above the regular rolls of the silk or linen, like the plume of a soldier's cap. Some of the women had many bracelets and bangles on their arms, chains of huge gold beads around their necks, and curious earrings of three or four cylinders of gold fastened to the ears by enormous hoops. These heavy pendants dragged down the lobes of the ears till it seemed as if the flesh would be torn through by their excessive weight.

Passing through the avenue Victor Hugo, which is the main street of the city, one morning, I overtook a crowd of boys who were following a rough and unkempt specimen of humanity, who carried a large iguana, which he had caught in the woods. He had tied the clumsy legs of the reptile across its back, and was carrying his captive by the tail. This immense lizard was as ugly a creature as I ever saw, about three feet long, with a black coarse skin divided into large diamond-shaped sections, a triangular head with lustreless eyes, and a cavernous mouth. His legs were long and thick, and ended in finger-shaped claws. The animal is not uncommon, is not at all dangerous to attack, and its flesh is said to be white and very much like chicken. This one was sold by its captor at the first butcher's shop, and for all I know we may have eaten it, in some of the highly seasoned ragouts of which we partook while on the island. It was at Martinique that some of the party made their acquaintance with the "swizzle," and in memory thereof brought home the swizzle-stick, a delicate twig with three or four small branches stripped of its bark, and prepared for the same use as the toddy-stick of former times. Of all beguiling drinks the "swizzle" is said to be the most delusive. It is apparently compounded of ice water and lime juice and lemonade, with a little pure rum, and a liberal allowance of sweet sirup. It tastes like sweet sherbet, and reminds one of the bazaars of Cairo and Damascus, but let not the unwary traveller quench his thirst as freely with this seemingly innocent beverage as he would among the temperate Mohammedans. The intoxicating quality of the alcohol is immensely increased by the fermentation of the sweetening, and those who ventured to test the chemical qualities of the "swizzle" by the personal analysis of more than one glass, were sorrowful and apologetic thereafter. Total abstinence is always a good rule where strong liquor is an ingredient in any drink, and especially useful in dealing with unknown mixtures.

This island was for a long time the residence of Père Labat, to whose chronicles I have already referred. He was a keen observer of all natural phenomena, as well as an expert judge of men. He tells how at the beginning of the rainy season the crabs, the turtles, the lizards, and the serpents leave the woods and go to the sea. After the latter have bathed there, they pass between underbrush which has thorns, to which they attach themselves by the collar, and leave their whole skin. They then hide in some hole or in the root of a tree until their new skin is sufficiently hardened to expose to the air. During these times, when they are obliged to remain in seclusion, they become very thin and feeble, but no one pities them under these or any circumstances. The time when the serpents are most dangerous is during the heat. Then one may hear them hiss to each other, and it is not a good plan to go hunting. The negroes scent these serpents as a dog would a hare.

"One morning," writes Labat, "I was in the woods with our men, one of whom was walking before me. Suddenly he stopped and said: 'My father, look at your feet, there is a serpent near here somewhere.' I asked him where, and he said: 'I do not see it, but I smell it,' and truly, I was sensible of a faint odor. A few moments later we discovered the serpent and killed it as is the custom. It was six feet long, and thick as a man's leg. I gave the body to some of our negroes, who easily disposed of it. I would have eaten some with them, for the meat is very nourishing, when not eaten too often, but for the fear of alarming the others of the party.

At another time I had the pleasure of seeing a snake swallow a pillory. This is a sort of rat, native to these islands, nearly white and much larger than the ordinary sized rat of Europe. As soon as the serpent had bitten the pillory, it climbed quickly into the branches of a tree at the foot of which the pillory struggled for about fifteen minutes and then died. The serpent then came down and rolled himself on the pillory, until he had arranged it with its front feet by its sides, and its back feet alongside of its tail, and after it was well laid out he took it by its head and sucked it little by little into his stomach, although it was quite difficult, for he was little and the pillory very big! It was his last meal, for after I had seen what I wanted to see I killed him."

There are many things to detain and interest the tourist at Martinique. The scenes and society of the island are different in many respects from those with which he becomes familiar in British colonies. The people do not regard themselves as temporary exiles hoping erelong to return to the mother country, as British colonial people generally do.. The French have made the island their home and are proud of its loveliness and prosperity. Martinique is inseparably associated with Napoleon as the birthplace of Josephine, and it has a large place in the history of the seventeenth-century conflicts between England and France.

We made sundry excursions to the interior of the island. One morning we drove for several hours up the heights to the village of Morne Rouge, two thousand feet above the sea, over a fine smooth road along which were shrines, and little chapels, and crucifixes, and statues, with lamps burning before them and numerous votive offerings. The road led us by the botanical garden, a choice and beautiful retreat from the noise of the town and the noonday heat of the sun. The river beside which the road is built for a portion of the way, was at this season a small stream, and its channel was filled with half-naked washerwomen who covered the rocks with garments after having reduced them to a pitiable condition by pounding them with stones. At the lower end of the town near to the outlet of the river is the market-place, a large open structure occupying a handsome square. It was full of people, a great proportion of whom were women in the gayest of costumes, and as noisy as parrots. The markets of any town are interesting, and give an idea of one phase of the life of a people; for what a nation eats and drinks has much influence upon what the nation does. Judging the natives of the Antilles by this rule, we may account for their unwarlike, good-natured, and passive character. Very little flesh is seen in the markets compared with the amount of fish and fruit. Nowhere else have I seen such fishes as swim among these islands. A painter would revel in their colors, scarlet and pink and green and gold and lilac and bronze and glistening silver. Their shapes are equally wonderful; long and sharp like a sword-blade, flat and oval like a griddle, circular as a ball and covered with sharp thorns, or round like a cane and mottled as a snake. Next come the vegetables and fruits — I have described them as I saw them at other islands, but Martinique seemed to have gathered from all the islands and added specialties of her own. The sellers were chiefly women, who squatted on their heels among their wares, while the restless many-colored crowd wound about among them, making a kaleidoscope at which one was never weary of looking. It was a change from this scene of clatter and confusion to the quiet of the botanical garden. This is about a mile from the town, and its natural features are sufficient to make it attractive. It lies along and within a ravine, whose lofty trees and tumbling water and deep quiet pools, and masses of vines and creepers, and confused assemblies of ferns and orchids and miniature palms, combine to give dense shade and coolness, and a sense of repose, which are most grateful after the glare and heat and noise of the market-place and the city streets. There are thickets of bamboo, and beautiful tamarinds, and wide-spreading ceiba trees, palms and palmistes in endless variety, great lianas and swinging vines, and parasites coiling around, and hanging from, and sitting upon the tree branches. The garden has a certain amount of care, and is better than any which I saw in the islands except those of the government houses of St. Vincent and Port of Spain, but with such a wealth of resources and a tropical climate, it is easy to imagine what wonders and beauties might be developed.

Leaving the garden, we climbed Morne Rouge over

well-made roads, with solid stone bridges and carefully prepared water channels in case of floods. The views were of indescribable loveliness, combining the grandeur of the mountains, the rich and varied greenery of the hills and cultivated slopes, and the deep blue of the distant sea. Now and then a cloud of mist swept for a few moments like a veil over the face of beauty, only to reveal after its passage a scene fresher and fairer than before. High above the neat and pretty villas, which form the village of Morne Rouge, is a steep slope which has been arranged for pilgrimage purposes. On the mountain side a succession of little chapels has been built — each of which contains some representation of the Passion of Our Lord. It is a Roman Catholic "Calvaire," and pious Romanists climb the mountain, sometimes on their knees, saying a prayer at each shrine. It is easier to get up with such intervals than to try to walk profanely to the top without resting. Even superstition has its compensations, and it may be added that the view on a fine day is enough recompense for the climb. The French islanders are better Christians after their kind, than the other inhabitants, but the amount of ignorant devotion to shrines and images is large. Besides the numerous little idols scattered along the roads, there is an immense "Christ" overlooking the bay, and on Morne d'Orange, south of the city, stands a huge white "Virgin of Sailors."

But there is one statue on Martinique which every traveller desires to see; the statue of Josephine in the Savane at Fort de France. A little steamer runs daily from St. Pierre to Fort de France. The town stands on a level plain and consists of wooden houses built along wide streets crossing at right angles. The park lies near the shore, and contains long rows of mango and tamarind trees, which bend over broad promenades. Enclosed in this double row of trees is the Savane, and there, encircled by majestic palms, fronting the sea, but with the face turned towards the valley where she was born, stands this beautiful memorial to one of the loveliest, and noblest, and most unfortunate women who ever lived. The family history has recently been given by M. Frederic Masson in the *Revue de Paris*, from which the following facts are translated. Mr. Ober published essentially the same statement, in his book upon the Caribbees.

In 1726 there came to Martinique a noble of Blaisois, named Gaspard-Joseph Tascher de la Pagerie. He belonged to an ancient and formerly very powerful family, but when Gaspard-Joseph landed in the West Indies the fortunes of his race had very much declined. He took good care, how-

STATUE OF JOSEPHINE—MARTINIQUE

ever, to have his claim to noble descent fully established. His sons obtained places at Court, but the eldest preferred to live at Martinique and obtained a subaltern position in the Royal Marines stationed at Martinique. In 1755, when a new war had broken out between France and England, the king sent to Martinique, as governor of the West Indian Islands, one François de Beauharnais, a gentleman who had held high positions in France. Exactly how it came about no one seems to know, but the Taschers, poverty-stricken and without influence, managed to raise the fortunes of the family through their women, who established themselves in the good graces of the new governor.

M. de Tascher's three daughters married well, and his son also made a good match through M. de Beauharnais, for Mlle. Rose-Claire Des Vergers de Sanois belonged to one of the richest and most influential colonial families. Young Gaspard-Joseph proved himself worthy of the good graces of the governor; he distinguished himself with conspicuous bravery when the English made a descent upon the island in 1763. On the 23d of June in that year his wife was delivered of a girl, which, five weeks later, was christened Marie-Joseph-Rose. This was Josephine. Between 1761 and 1791 six different priests held the parish of Trois-Flets, and this assisted in giving credence to the later rumors that Josephine's birth could not be proved by the parish registers. But there is no possible doubt either of her identity or of the exact date of her birth. In 1766 a terrible storm destroyed the plantation at Trois-Flets; it took M. de Tascher thirty years to obtain the means for rebuilding his house, and thus Josephine passed her childhood in and around the sugar-house, the only building which withstood the storm, and in which the family had established themselves. At the age of ten she was sent to the Convent of the Dames-de-la-Providence, at Fort Royal, where she remained until she was fifteen. She was an accomplished coquette even then; Captain Tercier, then stationed with his regiment at Martinique, flatters himself that she was not quite indifferent in his presence, and a young Englishman who rose afterward to high honors loved her so much that he never married because she refused him.

Madame Revandin, Josephine's aunt, had gone to France with M. de Beauharnais, over whom she exercised undue influence. Madame Revandin made up her mind that the Taschers de la Pagerie should profit by her good fortune. Why not marry young Alexander, the son of the Marquis de Beauharnais, to one of her nieces? Influenced as he was, the marquis writes, on behalf of his son, to M. Tascher for the hand of one of his daughters. Originally it was intended to marry Josephine's younger sister, Catherine-Désirée, to Alexander Beauharnais, but the young lady's death intervened. Josephine, then, was sent to France, and Madame Revandin spent twenty thousand francs on the girl's trousseau. Alexander was not very enthusiastic about the marriage, but the bans were published and the marriage took place within a month after the bride had landed.

The union was not a happy one. Alexander did not attempt to introduce his wife to society, and did nothing to assist her in completing her scant education and to improve her provincial ways. He complains, too, that she had the most absurd ideas of what conjugal affection should be like, required too much attention, and was jealous. Young Beauharnais — he was only nineteen at the time of his marriage — travelled to divert himself, and left his wife at home. He quarrelled with his wife's relatives, and accused Josephine of infidelity, and the latter retired to the Abbey of Panthemont, a convent which served as a kind of refuge for wives who were separated from their husbands, or were about to obtain a separation. Here she was for the first time made acquainted with the wiles of society.

Later M. de Beauharnais rendered the most complete apologies, acknowledging that Josephine was not at fault, and as a reconciliation seemed impossible, a separation was agreed upon. She returned, with her little daughter, Hortense, to the scenes of her childhood, and thus she wrote of this peaceful time so soon to be exchanged for a life as exciting and wonderful as any that woman ever knew: "Nature has strewn the banks of our rivers with flowers, and planted the freshest forests around our fertile borders. I cannot resist the temptation to breathe the pure aromatic odors wafted on the zephyr's wings. I love to hide myself in the green woods that skirt our dwelling; there I tread on flowers which exhale a perfume as rich as that of the orange grove, and more grateful to the senses. How many charms has this retreat for one in my situation." From this seclusion she came forth to ascend the throne of France and to adorn with her matchless charms the most brilliant court in the world. The keenest writer of fiction could not have conceived of anything more romantic than the making of this charming spot the birthplace of so distinguished a woman.

There was another illustrious Frenchwoman whose early years were passed in Martinique, who swayed for years the destinies of France. Madame de Maintenon, known before as Madame Scarron, grew up as Françoise d'Aubigné in this beautiful island. The story of her coming is romantic. Her parents were Protestants, living in Northern France, and hoping to improve their waning fortune and enjoy more religious freedom, removed to Martinique after the birth of their daughter. Soon after sailing the infant D'Aubigné became very ill and apparently died, and the captain insisted upon speedy burial in the sea and preparations were duly made. After some slight religious services just as the body was about to be thrown overboard, the mother, weeping violently, rushed forward and begged for one more look at her child, and passionately kissing the remains, she discovered some faint signs of life. The body was taken back to the cabin and efforts for resuscitation were crowned with success, and recovery was rapid.

Great was the joy of the pious parents, and earnest and devout their thanksgiving over recovering from the jaws of death their darling one. How little they knew what they were doing! This Protestant child, this child of prayer and faith, lived to be the scourge of the church of her parents; for few doubt that Madame de Maintenon was the chief agent in inducing Louis XIV. to revoke the edict of Nantes and inaugurate a persecution of untold blood and violence and horror, which nearly obliterated the Protestant name from the fair land of France.

With the memory of such great names it is not wonderful that French Creoles are proud of their heritage, and plan and labor for its prosperity.

XVI

BATTLES AMONG THE ISLANDS

BUCCANEERS OF THE SPANISH MAIN — COUNT DE GRASSE AND ADMIRAL RODNEY — A DECISIVE NAVAL BATTLE — THE SLOOP OF WAR DIAMOND ROCK

BEFORE leaving this part of the Caribbean Sea we ought to recall the naval history which has been enacted among the Windward Islands. The battles which Columbus fought with the natives were incidental to discovery and settlement; then came cruel wars for the conquest of the islands, and in order to grind gold in one way or another out of the islanders. The Roman Catholic church is responsible for much of this early fighting, for she had given the islands to the Spaniards by a papal bull, which no Protestant adventurer felt bound to respect, unless it was more than a *brutum fulmen*, and had ships and soldiers behind it. The freebooters and buccaneers of the Spanish Main were the terror of the dwellers on shore as well as of all who sailed the seas. Drake and his comrades were "pirates to the Spaniards" so writes Froude, "to be treated to a short shrift wherever found and caught. British seamen who fell into their hands were carried before the Inquisition at Lima or Carthagena and burnt at the stake as heretics." French privateers seized Tortuga near St. Domingo, and English, French, and Spanish all ravaged the seas in a wild anarchy.

Then came the period of French occupation, when nearly every island of the Antilles was settled by French colonists. Language, religion, customs, were all French, and the impress made in those days upon the islands has never been removed, though all save Martinique have passed from under French control. England determined that the Lesser Antilles should be hers, and fierce battles were fought for their possession; they were taken and retaken, and when the British under Cornwallis surrendered to Washington at Yorktown, French and Spanish allied to drive the British from the West Indies. Rodney, who was in command of the islands, had been ordered home to answer some charges which political enemies had brought against him; but when the news came that the Count De Grasse with his victorious fleet was about to sail for Martinique, Rodney was hurried back to his station with all the ships that he could muster. He arrived not a day too soon.

We shall let Froude tell the story of the naval

battle, one of the severest in English annals, of which he says that if it had been lost to England, "Gibraltar would have fallen and Hastings's Indian empire would have melted into air." De Grasse had refitted in the Martinique dock-yards. He had the finest ship then floating on the seas for his flag-ship, and his navy seemed invincible, a fleet with which he did not believe that even Rodney would venture to contend. "He held all the Antilles except St. Lucia — Tobago, Grenada, the Grenadines, St. Vincent, Martinique, Dominica, Guadeloupe, Montserrat, Nevis, Antigua, and St. Kitt's — a string of gems, each island large as or larger than the Isle of Man, rising up with high volcanic peaks clothed from base to crest with forest, carved into deep ravines and fringed with luxuriant plains. In St. Lucia alone, lying between St. Vincent and Dominica, the English flag still flew, and Rodney lay there in the harbor at Castries. On April 8, 1782, the signal came from the north end of the island that the French fleet had sailed. The air was light, and De Grasse was under the highlands of Dominica before Rodney came up with him. Both fleets were becalmed, and the English were scattered and divided by a current which runs between the islands." De Grasse failed to attack as he should have done, and only fired long shots which did considerable damage. Thus the fleets manœuvred for two days. "On the night of the eleventh Rodney made signal for the whole fleet to go south under press of sail. The French thought he was flying. He tacked at two in the morning, and at daybreak found himself where he wished to be, with the French fleet on his lee quarter. He had the advantage of the wind and could force a battle or decline it as he pleased.

"In number of ships the fleets were equal; in size and complement of crew the French were immensely superior, and besides the ordinary ships' companies they had twenty thousand soldiers on board who were to be used in the conquest of Jamaica. . . . With clear daylight the signal to engage was flying from the mast-head of the *Formidable*, Rodney's ship. At seven in the morning, April 12, 1782, the whole fleet bore down obliquely on the French line, cutting it directly in two. Rodney led in person. Having passed through and through and broken up their order, he tacked again, still keeping the wind. The French, thrown into confusion, were unable to reform, and the battle resolved itself into a number of separate engagements in which the English had the choice of position.

"Rodney in passing through the enemy's lines the first time had exchanged broadsides with the *Glorieux*, a seventy-four at close range. He had shot away her masts and bowsprit, and left her a bare hull, her flag however still flying, being nailed to a splintered spar. So he left her unable at least to stir, and after he had gone about came himself yard-arm to yard-arm with the superb *Ville de Paris*, the pride of France, the largest ship in the then world, which De Grasse commanded in person. One by one the French ships struck their flags or fought on till they foundered and went down. The *Ville de Paris* surrendered last, fighting desperately after hope was gone, till her masts were so shattered that they could not bear a sail and her decks above and below were littered over with mangled limbs. De Grasse gave up his sword to Rodney on the *Formidable's* quarterdeck. The gallant *Glorieux*, unable to fly, hauled down her flag, but not till the undisabled remnants of her crew were too few to throw the dead into the sea. Other ships took fire and blew up. Half the French fleet were either taken or sunk; the rest crawled away for the time, most of them to be picked up afterwards like crippled birds. On that memorable day was the English empire saved. The American colonies were lost; but England kept her West Indies." This naval battle settled the question of sovereignty in the Lesser Antilles.

Between Martinique and St. Lucia, but close to Martinique, there is a solitary rock, precipitous and apparently inaccessible, which claims our attention. It lies a mile south of the promontory known as Morne du Dimant, and is five hundred and seventy-five feet in height to its level top. There the English admiral, Sir Thomas Hood, once landed, and hoisted a garrison of dare-devil sailors with guns and provisions to the top of the rock. The crag was christened "His Majesty's sloop-of-war Diamond Rock"; and for nine months, from this sea-girt citadel, the British seamen startled the vessels of France and Spain, as they swept the neighboring seas with the guns of this strange man-of-war. The crew of Diamond Rock were finally compelled to yield to starvation what they never could have been obliged to surrender by force of arms, and the rock has ever since been carefully guarded against capture by the Frenchmen of Martinique.

XVII

ST. LUCIA

THE BEST LANDING PLACE IN THE CARIBBEES — TOWN OF CASTRIES — THE LOFTY AND WEIRD PITONS — TALES AND TRADITIONS

LEAVING Martinique after midnight, the early morning found us coasting along a most beautiful island, with forest-clad hills and deep, dark valleys lying between. The color effects were as wonderful here as at Dominica. The near slopes were covered with rich yellow-green fields of sugar-cane, the lofty peaks beyond were blue and purple, and the sea, which was hardly ruffled by the morning breeze, was like mother-of-pearl with streaks of silver where the currents changed its shining surface; far in the distance twin peaks were dimly seen through the haze above the nearer mountains, which on approach proved to be the two Pitons, the most remarkable of all the strange creations which we saw in this region of subterranean and volcanic forces.

St. Lucia is the largest of the islands that we visited, with the exception of Guadeloupe and

Trinidad. It has an area of one hundred and fifty thousand acres, a coast line of one hundred and fifty miles, and is forty-two miles long and twenty miles broad. From its lofty mountains, watered by frequent rains, numerous streams descend to the ocean; and at their mouths there are many bays and roadsteads for vessels. The island lies in 13 degrees 50 minutes north latitude and 60 degrees 58 minutes west longitude. It has between forty and fifty thousand inhabitants, the vast majority of whom are blacks. At the northeastern extremity of the island is a high cliff detached from the mainland, where Admiral Rodney, a century ago, established a signal station, and from which he watched the manœuvres of the French fleet whose headquarters were at Martinique. Passing through a narrow strait between two lofty headlands, the steamer entered one of the best harbors in the West Indies, and was soon alongside a fine stone wharf. This was the only place during our voyage among the Caribbees, where we were able to land from a gang-plank and without the service of a small boat. Large sums of money have been spent here by the British government to deepen the harbor, and make the place a coaling station for the British navy and for the Royal mail steamers. Here is the town of Castries, named in honor of the French marshal

De Castries in 1785, when the French held the place.

The ruins of an ancient fortress crown the heights of Morne Fortune upon the southern side of the town, and a few British soldiers showed us by their presence to whom the island now belongs.

Castries has been built upon made ground, at the foot of the heights, and is occupied chiefly by blacks, who live in long rows of little wooden houses with corrugated iron roofs. There is a handsome market, neat and well supplied; a pretty botanical garden with a rich variety of trees and tropical plants, with its ground full of snake holes; and a comfortable reading room and library of about a thousand volumes. The people speak English, and the whites all live upon the hills around the harbor; for the low ground is unhealthy, and has a bad reputation for fevers.

Here, as at St. Thomas, we saw women coaling the vessels. Their short skirts and naked arms and shoulders revealed brawny limbs and chests on which the muscles stood out as on a sculptor's bronze when, with the great baskets of coal upon their heads, they mounted the gang-planks of the vessels at the pier. They sang a monotonous chant as they worked in the grime and dust of the coal breakers or marched in single file across the wharf to throw in their loads. Even the coal dust could hardly make them blacker than they came from nature's hand, and there was little except their arrowy uprightness to differentiate them from the animals among which they labored. We were not disposed to linger at Castries, though we had invitations to visit in the island. We were becoming rather impatient for a more extended civilization than this island afforded, and were already thinking of Barbados and Trinidad.

The voyage from Castries to St. Vincent was one of our finest experiences. We coasted the leeward side of St. Lucia till sundown, watching peak after peak of a superbly foliated mountain chain with admiration, till the climax came in the wonderful Pitons, two immense cones 2720 and 2680 feet in sheer height from the water's edge. The loftiest one seemed to be almost as difficult of ascent (except for its ice) as the last three thousand feet of the Matterhorn in the Zermatt valley, which it much resembles in shape. But their forms change as the vessel passes by these wonderful peaks, and so also do their colors change under the varying atmosphere. At their foot a beautiful bay opens, where a green plantation and the white houses of a little hamlet relieve the severity of the landscape. Above and behind this bay, however, rises the sombre mountain of the Souffrière, a smoking sulphur vent whose blue fumes mingle with gray mists and rain-clouds, which are forever hovering about the mountains. No description can do justice to the fantastic and awe-inspiring picture which these towering masses present. Even photographs fail to convey the atmosphere of the scene, but the landscape painter has here, as elsewhere among these islands, a noble subject, in form and color unique and wonderful, for his study and reproduction upon the canvas.

History or tradition tells a story of three sailors who tried to climb these awful steeps, watched with breathless interest by their less adventurous comrades. As they neared the summit one and another were seen to fall suddenly, as if stricken by an enemy, and the third also, just as he was waving the flag in triumph on the summit, fell backwards a corpse. These repeated disasters were ascribed to the deadly bite of the fer-de-lance, that dreaded serpent which infested St. Lucia in past years, but whose descendants have been nearly extirpated by the mongoose, which is now in turn voted a nuisance by the planters of the island. A practical view of the tale, with the Pitons in sight, lessened our faith in the tradition of the climbing and bitten sailors. Even with the aid of a powerful field-glass, it would be quite impossible to look through the dense thickets and watch the progress of any climber on the seaward side of the Pitons; and so, though the tale is illustrative of the reckless courage of the seamen of former times, and the dreadful enemies which lay in wait for early travellers in St. Lucia, we can only offer it as a bit of sensational literature with rather a slight foundation of fact.

St. Lucia has, however, a wonderful record of battles on land and sea which well attests the bravery of the peoples who fought for supremacy in the Spanish Main in the seventeenth and eighteenth centuries. In 1605 sixty-seven colonists landed at St. Lucia and took possession in the name of James the First of England. Two months later the Caribs drove them into the sea. It was more than thirty years before another attempt at settlement was made by a British colony and with the same result. In 1642 the king of France, who had assumed the sovereignty of a large part of the West Indies, sold St. Lucia to two Frenchmen for about eighty thousand dollars. These Frenchmen established a colony, which was attacked and conquered in 1664 by a party of English from Barbados; but the treaty of Breda gave the island back to France. St. Lucia changed hands many times, and was also a neutral ground during the next fifty years. From 1756 to 1782, France and England fought

THE PITONS—ST. LUCIA

ST. LUCIA

again and again for the possession of St. Lucia. The greatest and most decisive conflict was on April 12, 1782, a naval battle which I have already described, when Admiral Rodney almost annihilated the French fleet and took De Grasse, the French admiral, a prisoner; for which service he was made a peer of the realm and received a pension of two thousand pounds for himself and his heirs. The French government was restored by treaty in 1784, and under the Directory, in February, 1794, General Ricard, the French governor of St. Lucia, abolished negro slavery throughout the French Antilles, forty years before English emancipation in the West Indies, and seventy years sooner than the abolition of slavery in our own republic. Strange as it seems, this blow for freedom was struck from Paris by the leaders of the French Revolution.

Bloody battles continued to be fought between the French and English for the ownership of St. Lucia, from 1794 to 1803. What the English gained by fighting, was often given back to the French by treaty. In the famous battles of 1796, the negroes united with the French and made a gallant struggle, for they were fighting to retain the freedom which the French had given them. It was, however, in vain, and the island, after more than a century and a half of warfare for its possession, became English soil. The English soon lost all interest in what had cost them so dear, and only within a few years has the English government awaked to the value and importance of St. Lucia among her West Indian colonies. It is a most valuable island with fine harbors, full of tropical productions, and with sulphur mines in the Souffrière which could supply the powder factories of the world. Those who are interested in natural phenomena should visit these volcanoes and read in Humboldt's "Personal Narrative," book fifth, his descriptions of the Antilles and their natural history, and especially those pages which treat of the great eruptions of 1812, which culminated in the tremendous outbreak of the Souffrière of St. Vincent — whither now the *Madiana* had set her course.

XVIII

ST. VINCENT AND THE GRENADINES

A SUPERB AMPHITHEATRE — OUTBURST OF A VOLCANO — MAKING ARROWROOT — BARGAINING FOR A BABY — A LITTLE ARCHIPELAGO

RUNNING southward through the night, we crossed the channel south of St. Lucia, and in the morning reached the next link in the chain of the Caribbee Islands, and came to anchor off St. Vincent. It has been said that four islands among the Caribbees realize one's ideals — Guadeloupe, Dominica, Martinique, and St. Vincent. The first is vast, grand, and gloomy; the second sombre in its mountains, but breaking out into smiling tracts of cultivated land; the third combines features of the first two, and adds the element of a large and picturesque population; while St. Vincent has all the natural wonders and beauties of the other three, and a certain air of delicate culture which is entirely its own.

We were anchored in a lovely bay with a fort crowning the headland on our right, and facing Kingstown. The town is situated in a superb amphitheatre which rises from the water with its red-roofed houses showing through palm groves, and a few fine stone structures, among which are churches of five denominations of Christians. Behind these buildings are the botanical gardens and the governor's house overlooking all the town. St. Vincent is a single peak, with no outlying rocks or islets. It is larger than it seems, being seventeen miles long and ten miles broad, with an area of one hundred and thirty-one square miles and a population of nearly fifty thousand. A mountain ridge divides the island, and here, at the height of a mile, is the vast crater of Morne Garon, which was the scene of a tremendous eruption in 1812, when the earthquakes which for two years had terrified the South American coast and the West India Islands, had culminated in an explosion which at Caracas buried in a moment ten thousand people; wrought ruin along the whole line of the Andes, and ended in an awful outburst from the Souffrière of St. Vincent, whose dust darkened the sun for an entire day, and spread over a hundred miles of sea and land. This eruption changed the appearance of the island, and seemed to have destroyed its eastern end. The present crater, formed at that time, is half a mile in diameter and five hundred feet deep. The old crater is now a beautiful blue lake, walled in by ragged cliffs to a height of eight hundred feet.

ST. GEORGES—ISLAND OF GRENADA

But the devastation of April, 1812, has not been repeated. The volcano did its work and gave vent to the hidden forces of a continent, and beneficent Nature has repaired the ruin and made the island more beautiful than ever. We landed from boats at a little wharf built out from the sandy beach which curves from the northern headland around to the southern promontory, and found Kingstown a neat and pleasant town. Some of the party made friends with residents, and were invited to bring their pajamas and make an interval in the voyage under the palm and cinnamon trees with tropical company and its delights; but they were loyal to their companions and, though sorely tempted, followed the example of Ulysses without being tied to the mast or having their ears plugged with wool after the style of the Homeric hero.

We found that the stone buildings along the seashore were occupied by a police station and government stores. Three streets, broad and lined with good houses, are laid out fronting the water, and these are intersected at right angles by other streets which run back to the foot-hills, from which roads lead into the mountain regions and around the shore to the north and south. Along these streets are rows of palms whose columnar stems are crowned with waving fronds, so that the town lies in a beautiful crescent leaning back against the verdurous hills, itself half-hidden in a lovely grove, while far above and beyond rises the dark mountain around whose torn and rent edges the clouds are ever floating. Froude was reminded of Norway by the scene, and it is true that St. Vincent has some of the characteristics of those bright wooden-built towns which the traveller finds upon the steep sides of the dark fjords of that northern land, and here nature is so lavish of her treasures that the sentiment of grandeur is quite overcome by the softer beauties of the landscape. In the centre of the picture as seen from the roadstead is the handsome government house. It stands at the highest point of a richly stocked and well-cultivated botanical garden, where we saw plantations of pineapples, the cinnamon, clove, camphor and nutmeg, mahogany, ceiba, cottonwood and many wildwood trees, and a great variety of plants and flowers. The main room of the government house is a wide hall reaching from front to rear, furnished and used for both salon and dining-rooms, with bedrooms opening out on either side. Beyond these is a large and deep tank for bathing, and still further on are the servants' offices and farm buildings. Loaded with flowers and fruits we descended to the town, passing upon our way an arrowroot plantation with its simple mill. The root grows in fields which are planted as corn is planted for fodder. When sufficiently grown it is dug up and carted to the mill. The tubers are there broken off, ground, washed, and strained, and the mass is allowed to settle for a few days. The product is then placed on wire-work frames of different-sized meshes, to dry. It gradually sifts down from the coarse upper frame to the lowest fine netting, and by that time it has become dry and is ready to be barrelled and shipped. It now brings five dollars a barrel, or about eight cents a pound. Not many years ago it brought from forty to sixty cents. This high price led many into the business and like most West Indian industries, this has been overdone, with the usual result.

We visited several of the island schools and found that the process of teaching was largely oral, the whole class reciting in unison with the teacher and memorizing their lessons. The children were, of course, all black, and seemed bright and attentive, and the teachers were painstaking, but education does not appear to elevate the people. They are not idle, dissipated, or wicked, but only lacking in ambition. Like most of the negroes in the islands, they prefer to be governed rather than to govern. They do not know how to rule, and they do know how to serve; and in the service of a superior race they are kindly, and fairly faithful where they are well treated, now that there is no slavery. Their morals cannot be judged by the standard of white communities, and it seems to be almost impossible to apply the notions of civilization to them. As I came into the town, a number of negro women were sitting in front of their cottages, while the naked children played around. One little fellow of perhaps five years was carrying a large pail upon his head, followed by a smaller child bearing a cocoanut, and a toddling two-year-old bringing up the rear with an empty tomato can neatly balanced on his growth of black wool. They marched in file, back and forth, without once shaking off their little burdens, and were thus learning to carry those huge loads upon their heads without mishap or apparent effort, which never cease to astonish the traveller. One of the women held up to me by one leg a beautiful specimen of black humanity, and in jest I offered five francs for the child. "You give ten and have him," was the unexpected reply, to which I at once demurred. The mother was evidently in earnest, and urged: "Take him to New York and he grow big and wait on rich gentleman; plenty same here; say ten, gentleman; see I give him for ten." Had it been a monkey, I must have surrendered, but the risk and responsibility for a soul bought for ten francs was too much for me, and I was sorry for my jesting offer.

Our voyage to the southward was drawing towards its end. We steamed from St. Vincent past the Grenadines, which are a group of long, low islands varying from mere rocks to islands having an area of eight or ten thousand acres. Most of them are inhabited by a contented and fairly prosperous population. Becquia is the largest and nearest to St. Vincent. It is six miles long and a mile wide, and its highest hill is nearly a thousand feet above the sea. Balliceaux, Battowia, Mustique, Canonau, Carriacou, and Union Island are some among many owned perhaps by one person or firm. Cattle and sheep are raised on these islands, but the only communication between them and the larger islands is by boats. Grenada is the farthest south of the Caribbee Islands and is one of the most beautiful of the chain. It is eighteen miles long and seven broad, with lofty and extinct volcanic craters, and a picturesque lake more than two miles in circumference and two thousand feet above the sea. We were sorry not to visit its capital, Georgetown, also called St. George's, with its fine harbor, walled fort, pretty red-roofed houses on the hillside, and churches with tapering spires. There are many monkeys in the mountains of Grenada, and great is said to be the sport of hunting them, and there is also agreeable human society in the town. But we were bound for Barbados, and all night long we rolled, steaming easterly against a head wind and sea, to the temporary discomfort of some of the passengers. Morning found us at anchor in front of Bridgetown among a crowd of vessels, with the green and white island of Barbados densely dotted with little cabins among sugar-cane fields, extending as far as the eye could reach.

XIX

BARBADOS

A SCENE OF BUSY LIFE — SWARMS OF PEOPLE — BRIDGE-
TOWN AND THE ICE HOUSE — CRISIS IN THE SUGAR
TRADE — BENEFICENT EFFECTS OF BRITISH RULE

THE winter sky was cloudless, and the winter sun in the roadstead of Barbados was as hot as the July sun in New York. The thermometer in the shade marked seventy-four degrees at sunrise; at noon, in the sun, it rose to one hundred and twenty, and no white person walked in the streets of Bridgetown without an umbrella. But a steady trade wind blew from the ocean all day long, and made a quiet existence in shady places comfortable. From the deck of the steamer we looked upon a handsome city whose dazzling whiteness was relieved here and there by clusters of green palms, while beyond lay undulating fields of sugar-cane, among which little cottages were thickly planted. Carlisle bay was full of vessels. Great steamers from Europe and South America were loading and discharging cargoes into lighters, while four-masted schooners and other sailing vessels from the United States, from Canada, Denmark, and Norway, lay moored in the roads. Our own White Squadron and war vessels of several European nations added impressiveness to the marine picture, and multitudes of fishing smacks, with cargoes of flying-fish, skimmed over the dancing waves. Rowboats manned by half a dozen negroes plied to and fro, between the little artificial harbor where small vessels could lie alongside, and the larger craft which were anchored in the bay.

The scene was full of busy life and quite in contrast with our peaceful and lonely anchorages for a month past at the beautiful islands on our southern course. It was evident that we had come to a sort of maritime exchange, a port of call where goods and passengers were transshipped, where vessels stopped for mails and supplies, a centre of trade and commerce. Everything bore the impress of Great Britain. The negroes spoke no foreign patois, but chattered in pure English; the boats were huge and strong, with heavy oars, such as one sees in Liverpool and Hull; officials in uniform were numerous, and on landing we walked over English roads, well swept and watered, and among shops and buildings which reminded us of a dozen English seaports. In an hour we saw more white people

NELSON SQUARE—BARBADOS

in Bridgetown than we had seen in all the other Windward Islands. There were many heavy carriages and carts in the streets, most of which had come from England, with now and then a lighter vehicle which betrayed its Yankee origin. Had it not been for the throngs of black people, we might have imagined ourselves in a town of the British isles. But this feature of Barbadian life dispelled all such illusions. There is no part of the British empire, indeed no country in the world, which is more thickly peopled than Barbados, and of course the vast majority of the people are blacks. It is estimated that nine-tenths of the two hundred thousand inhabitants are of this race, and they swarm in the streets and over the roads and seem to crowd the country with their cabins. There are more than a thousand people to every square mile of the island, and when I add that less than one-fifteenth of the land is uncultivated, and out of this small area much must be deducted for houses and other buildings, for public and private parks, and for burial places, the crowded condition of the black population will be apparent. They multiply too with rapidity, and they stay where they are born. Hence the question of support is an ever-present problem. Wages at the time of our visit were at the starvation point, if there can be any such point in a tropical country where nature does so much for man and requires so little. I was told again and again, that day laborers worked for a shilling a day, and that even at that rate there were many who could not get employment. With the terrible depression of sugar, which is the main agricultural product of the island, the outlook for the laborer is very gloomy. While I am writing these lines a press despatch is handed to me, which reads as follows: —

"The West Indian sugar trade is passing through a serious crisis. In Barbados the crop now reaping is very far below the average, in some cases less than half. Many estates are in the hands of the official assignee, in chancery, and the number is increasing daily. The present deplorable condition of affairs is regarded generally as only a beginning. The colony is over populated, money is scarce, the number of unemployed alarmingly great, and the wages small. Agricultural laborers can now be engaged for twenty cents a day. Women get only twelve cents. Thousands of both sexes are unable to find employment at even these rates. The government of Barbados has taken steps to assist emigration. It has sent commissioners to inspect several of the neighboring colonies to give form to a scheme of colonization. The news from St. Lucia and Trinidad is that many estates in these colonies have been abandoned. At Antigua,

Dominica, St. Kitt's, St. Vincent, and generally through the Greater and Lesser Antilles the same state of affairs exists. On several islands public meetings have been held and resolutions have been adopted for transmission to the secretary of state for colonies, directing his attention to the impending ruin of the sugar industry in the British West Indies. The secretary has been asked to approach France and Germany with a view to ending their system of bounties to the growers of beet sugar and, failing in this, to have a duty imposed on all sugars imported into England from the bounty countries."

As a natural result of such hard times, fears were expressed of riot and crime should this state of things be long continued. If such danger exists, I am bound to say that there were no visible signs of a coming storm. The streets were full of busy crowds, the markets were heaped with all sorts of food and fruits, the shops displayed goods from every part of the globe and were thronged with buyers, and the gardens and fields were alive with industrious and cheerful men and women. There were no anti-rent and labor demonstrations with banners and mottoes, nor gatherings of sullen and discontented workmen. The negro lives by the day and is easily satisfied; and he has none of that chronic dissatisfaction with the existing order of things, which breeds so much wickedness and misery among what we call "the masses" in our continental and highly civilized communities.

Bridgetown has fine public buildings and many elegant residences. The houses are built of the limestone which has been reared by coral insects over the old volcanic formations of the island. It is easily worked, and so white that under the bright sun there is always a glare, and so easily pulverized that with the prevailing trade winds there are always clouds of dust on the highways, and in those streets which are not constantly watered. The best part of the place is occupied by the governor, the bishop, the attorney-general, and the barracks and parade ground of the English troops, but there are also several long avenues shaded by rows of palms on which new and pretty villas stand in richly cultivated gardens. Some older and larger residences occupy beautiful parks adorned with superb tropical trees. These handsome places are in striking contrast to the crowded rows of negro cabins which line the road far out towards the cane fields. A railway runs across the island, the only one in the Caribbees, and by this conveyance some of our party made a visit to Codrington College, a long-established and honorable seat of learning. On Trafalgar Square stand a small monument to Nelson and a big banyan tree which rivals in size and age the one in the park at Basse Terre on the island of St. Kitt's, though its position in a crowded city square makes it appear inferior to the Kittefonian tree.

The great resort for travellers is the Ice House, a spacious hotel whose lower story is devoted to shops, and its second floor to dining and public rooms. Here, meals in which flying-fish form a prominent item are constantly going on. A blackboard at the entrance displays the bill of fare for the different hours of the day, and the tables are always thronged. The public rooms are also full of people talking sugar and freights, and reading the tissue paper telegrams from all parts of the world, which are posted on the walls. These occupations are enlivened by the continual serving, by black waiters in white clothes, of cooling drinks in which the "swizzle" is always prominent. A few miles from town, not far from the shore, is the Marine hotel, a well-kept house under the charge of a Maine landlord, where many Americans spend a portion of the winter months. The climate is healthy and the diversions of sailing and fishing, added to excellent society if one has proper introductions, make this place a pleasant and desirable resort. Here some of our companions during the voyage had planned to spend a few weeks, intending to return by other steamers and different routes, when the winter winds had ceased to blow and spring had begun its verdant procession through the United States. A few of them had bicycles, on which they proposed to make tours over the excellent roads of the island; others were to visit friends in Barbados, and a few, tired of voyaging, were inclined to exchange their cabins in the *Madiana* for the large rooms and the extended freedom which are to be found in a good hotel on land. We were not yet ready, however, for city life, with railroads, and street cars, and telephones, even in such a pleasant climate, and so, with the majority of the party, having tried the cuisine of the Ice House, and added largely to our stock of curiosities, beads, and canes and shells, polished turtle-backs and fans of gorgeous plumes, we were ready to embark once more, for the voyage to Trinidad.

Before we go, a few facts about Barbados should be recorded. The Portuguese claim to have discovered the island in 1518, and to have given it the name, which means "bearded," because at that time there was a large growth of banyan trees on the island whose masses of fibrous roots hanging from the branches resembled huge beards swaying in the wind. Barbados is the most easterly of the Caribbees, lying in latitude thirteen degrees north, and longitude fifty-nine and one-half degrees west. It is from eighteen to twenty miles long, and about twelve miles wide, and contains one hundred and sixty-six square miles, nearly one hundred and seven thousand acres, of which as I have said less than one-fifteenth is uncultivated. The greater part of the surface is a rolling country, though in the northeastern part of the island, which is called Scotland, there are some high hills, called Mounts Hillaby and Boscobella. An abundant rainfall secures the region from drought, in spite of its scanty water-courses, and the extreme fertility of the soil assures abundant harvests. If the entire population had not devoted their energies to the production of sugar, there would be less poverty among the blacks and a prosperity among the planters which the rise and fall of the sugar market would not greatly disturb. The island has always been under British rule, and it shows the beneficent effects of an undisturbed and firm government through more than two centuries. During this period there are records of slight shocks of earthquake and of several destructive tornadoes; but, upon the whole, Barbados may be reckoned as one of the safest, healthiest, and, from a social point of view, the most agreeable of the Windward Islands. We spent a day at Bridgetown, upon the return voyage, and left the place with pleasant memories of our brief visits.

XX

TRINIDAD

THE DRAGON'S MOUTH AND THE GULF OF PARIA — DISCOVERY BY COLUMBUS — THREE FEARFUL FIRES — RAILWAYS, STEAMSHIPS, AND ACTIVE COMMERCE — FAMOUS GARDENS

SEVENTEEN hours of continuous steaming in a southwesterly direction from Barbados brought us within sight of the blue mountains of Trinidad. We passed by daylight along the northern coast, and arrived at the narrow entrance of the Gulf of Paria, known as Boca Drago, or the Dragon's Mouth. Our course was along lofty hills rising from the water's edge, which were clothed from sea to sky in dense, dark forests. The volcanic appearance which marked the Caribbean Islands is gone, and Trinidad looks like a part of a continent. Suddenly a narrow passage opened through the mountain wall, with a little rocky island, whitened by sea-birds, in its midst. Far out on the horizon beyond the misty clouds which hovered over the sea, could be discovered the continent of

GOVERNOR'S HOUSE—TRINIDAD

South America. Through a maze of currents, which would have made the passage difficult to a sailing vessel, the steamer forced its way, and in a short time we had passed among a few low wooded islands into the vast Gulf of Paria, the great watery plain where the floods of the Orinoco spread themselves before mingling with the sea. The change was marvellous; instead of the bright blue ocean we were ploughing a yellow sea, waveless and blazing with the reflection of a tropical sun. The hills of Trinidad rose in the east, westward the sky met the water, while a low shore could be seen in the far south fringed with mangroves and palms.

We had come into the gulf by the northern passage; the southern, by which Columbus entered on his third voyage, lies opposite and is called the Boca Sierpe, or Serpent's Mouth. Here after a long and trying voyage, the great navigator had found land again, and in fulfilment of a vow to name the first land after the Holy Trinity, he called the island Trinidad. He found groves of palm trees and noble forests and abundant springs and streams, though he had supposed that so near the equator nature would be parched and sterile. It was January, and he likens the climate to that of Southern Spain. Equally did the people please him, for he describes them as "people all of good stature, well made and of very graceful bearing, with much and smooth hair." They were fairer than the other Indians; their chiefs wore little clothing, and the women none at all; they were armed with bows and arrows and carried shields of hide. The Spaniards came again and again to Trinidad, and made its natives slaves, and it was not until a century had passed that Sir Walter Raleigh sailed into the Gulf of Paria, and landed at La Brea, which is now celebrated as the shipping place for the great Pitch Lake, and tarred his ship with the black bitumen which now supplies the material for American city pavements. Two centuries of cruelty and conflict between Spain and France and England succeeded, during which the natives suffered most of all, till, in 1797, the island became an English possession. The Carib population has long since died out, and thousands of negroes and East Indian coolies have taken their place. All sorts of people resort to Trinidad for purposes of gain — English, French, Spaniards, Americans, Portuguese, Chinese, gather there, and the island is prosperous. Not more than a quarter of the soil is under cultivation, but its fertility is great and the yield is large. Each year sees new plantations of indigo, and coffee, and cocoa, and sugar-cane; and even the coolies get rich and go back to India with bags of gold and silver, as the results of their five or ten years of toil in exile.

When the anchor of the *Madiana* went down into the Gulf of Paria and we steamed ahead to bring it to a hold, the water became as muddy as the Mississippi. A steam launch soon came to carry the passengers ashore, and on our way thither we passed a dismantled and rusting hulk moored before the town, and also a river steamer with its huge stern-wheel. This was the freight and passenger steamer in which one of our company, who had entertained us with his mandolin, his monkey bought at St. Kitt's, and his photographic views, was to ascend the Orinoco. I have seen him since the voyage, and his tales of the dangers and delights of the way made me long for a chance to go up this river and the still larger Amazon, and see nature and man in these fresh routes of travel.

Port of Spain was a curious compound of English, French, and Spanish buildings placed on broad streets or around tree-planted squares, with tramways along the chief avenues, dirty gutters and hundreds of disgusting black and gray buzzards, gobbling up refuse or roosting on the trees. I use the past tense in speaking of the town, for a few days after we left the place, a fire broke out and spread rapidly, destroying the business portion of the town and entailing a loss of four millions of dollars. It was only through the efforts of the marines of the American men-of-war *New York*, *Cincinnati*, and *Raleigh* that a more terrible loss of property and of life was averted. The marines to the number of two hundred and fifty rendered prompt and efficient service with their fire hose, which was taken ashore in the ships' boats. This is the third great fire which has occurred here in the past dozen years. A fire broke out in the Union Club House on the morning of January 28, 1884, and in a short time the whole southeastern portion of the town was in ruins. The principal hotel and the largest dry-goods establishment were entirely destroyed. The loss was estimated at more than $400,000. At that time there was no fire department in Port of Spain, and the flames subsided only when everything before them was consumed.

There was a second serious fire in Port of Spain early in the morning of February 15, 1891, which destroyed many lives and much valuable property. In a very picturesque esplanade called Marine Square was located a hotel, kept by a Venezuelan gentleman and patronized largely by Venezuelans. On the night of February 14 this hotel had about fifty guests, who retired to bed between eleven o'clock and midnight. The fire had its origin in this hotel at about three o'clock of the following morning, and destroyed the principal staircase leading to the street, thus cutting off the escape of many of the boarders. The hotel was composed of stone and wood, and consisted of a basement, upper floor, and attic. Most of the men lodgers succeeded in getting out, but in the attic were located three Venezuelan women, — Senorita Maria Echevarria and Senoras Rosa Echevarria and Rosaria de Osio. There were also nine children and two servants sleeping in this attic. When these persons learned that the building was on fire, they rushed madly to the staircase, only to find it gone. Thousands of spectators who had gathered in the streets witnessed the terrifying spectacle of these mothers throwing their children and themselves from the attic windows. A gentleman, Geronimo Fagasin, who had also been sleeping in the attic, threw himself out of the window and broke his neck in the fall. Of those who fell, only one survived, the little Concha Osio, four years old. The others all died from their injuries. The fire meanwhile had spread to the adjoining buildings, and in a short time something like $200,000 worth of property was destroyed. In the fire of March, 1895, though an immense amount of property was burned, fortunately no lives were lost, but many persons were rendered homeless and financially ruined, and the commerce of the place was seriously crippled.

There is an extensive carrying trade between Port of Spain and Venezuela. Gold and other produce of the latter country are brought to Trinidad for reshipment, and goods from Europe and elsewhere are sent to Trinidad and re-exported thence to Venezuela. Port of Spain is the only harbor of any commercial importance on the island, and it is also regarded as one of the best in the West Indies. Eighteen steamers a month from Liverpool, London, and Southampton give Port of Spain exceptionally good means of communication with England and with the other West Indian islands. In addition, four steamers of the French line, two of the Quebec and Gulf line, two of the Atlantic and West Indian line from the United States, and two of the Dutch line run every month. There are also seven steamers running between the island and Venezuela. The first railway in the colony, from Port of Spain to Arnia, sixteen miles, was opened in 1876. From St. Joseph, a station on the line six miles from Port of Spain, a line has been built to San Fernando, twenty-nine miles, and Prince's Town, thirty-six miles. The total length of railway open on December 31, 1890, was fifty-four and a quarter miles, the whole of which was constructed at a total cost of £602,638, and is owned by the government. Coast steamers ply three times a week from Port of Spain to San Fernando and on to Cedros in the southwestern corner of the island, a total distance of sixty miles.

The government house stands out of town, in large grounds at the foot of the mountains. In front and around it are the famous botanical gardens. We had seen nothing equal to them in the West Indies. Every known species of palm tree, from the tall cocoa palm laden with fruit, to the traveller's palm whose stems hold a tumblerful of refreshing water, were growing here. Nutmeg, cinnamon, and other spice trees, immense ceibas with their buttressed trunks, flamboyants and almonds, orange orchards, coffee and pineapple plantations filled the air with fragrance, and masses of flowers delighted the eye with rich and varied colors. Huge vines hung from some of the largest trees and orchids clung to trunks and branches. It was a paradise of vegetation, rank and rich, yet under careful and intelligent supervision. We spent a morning of delight among these natural wonders and beauties, and then strolled by pleasant roads to the beautiful Savannah, and lunched at a new and well-appointed hotel on one of the streets which bound this great pleasure ground of Trinidad.

XXI

HINDUS AT TRINIDAD

CONTRAST OF RACES — COOLIE APPRENTICESHIP, LABOR
AND LIFE — A COLLECTION OF LIVING CURIOSITIES —
HINDU PRIEST, ACCAWAI INDIANS, AND COOLIE BELLE

ONE of the most interesting excursions which the traveller can make in Trinidad is to the coolie villages. The coolie village in connection with Port of Spain is about three miles from the town. The road thither is lined with bamboo thickets and rows of palm trees, and their shade is appreciated in this tropical region, where the direct rays of the sun are painful and dangerous. We drove through uncleanly suburbs where black vultures were feeding upon garbage, and soon came to the village. It is a collection of shanties by the roadside made of boards or of palm thatch supported on bamboo props. In front of each were men, women, and children; a totally different race from the negroes or the black West Indians. Clothed in his long white linen gown, with a turban on his head, or with nothing on but the scarf twisted

HINDUS AT TRINIDAD 185

about his loins, the Hindu bears himself with dignity and reserve. His features are delicate and clear-cut, his manners are those of a civilization of which the negro knows nothing, and which indicates the sway of mind over matter. He may be a degraded heathen and know little more than the African, but he does not thus impress the visitor. He has the gravity of the sphinx, and an aristocratic bearing which is out of harmony with his environment. One instinctively connects the negro with the animal creation; it would be impossible to imagine the Hindu as anything but a man. Even when seated cross-legged before a little charcoal furnace fashioning silver and gold ornaments out of coins, or carrying loads, or working in the fields, there is something in shape or movement or expression that indicates mental power, a descent from a cultured ancestry, a superiority to present conditions. Much of this is doubtless due to the contrast which is presented in such a place as Port of Spain between the noisy and loose-mannered negroes of the town and the silent, self-contained coolies, who dwell apart in their own village; but circumstances will not wholly account for such marked differences as are seen in the races.

There are many thousand of these coolies in

Trinidad, and upon the whole the arrangements under which they emigrate and work in the island are beneficial to employer and employed. They are brought from Hindustan at the expense of the colony under the care of government agents, and are of course well cared for and fed during the voyage. On arrival those who are in good condition are apprenticed to owners who desire them, for five years. Families are not allowed to be separated except in the case of children who are over fifteen years of age. They are bound by law to work nine hours a day for two hundred and eighty days in the year, and receive the regular rate of wages. The law punishes the coolie for wilful idleness, and the employer for any fraud in his dealings with the laborer. For the two first years a part of their payment consists of rations, but for the rest of their time they are paid in cash. Each estate employing coolies is obliged to provide a hospital which is under the inspection of a medical visitor, and all the labor arrangements are subject to the inspection of a government agent who visits the estates constantly and reports each week to the agent-general of immigrants. He in turn reports to the governor, who has absolute authority to cancel the contract and remove any or all of the coolies from an estate. The system is a good one, provided only that the agents and the governor are of high character, and faithful in the discharge of their duties; and so far as I could learn, it has worked well in Trinidad.

When the five years of indenture are ended, the coolie can make a new contract for a year or he can work for whomsoever he chooses. After he has been in the colony ten years, he can claim a free passage home to India, or he is allowed to receive instead of that claim a government grant of ten acres of land. The coolies have usually preferred the former, though some have settled permanently in the island, and others have returned for a second term of service, bringing friends and relatives with them. Though these Hindus are all low caste, yet they do not amalgamate to any extent with the other blacks. They dwell by themselves as far as possible, they have a priest of their own religion, and they live a simple family life; they are jealous of their marital rights, extremely fond of their children, frugal in their expenditures, and as well behaved as any class of the community. They live mostly in the open air, for in the climate of Trinidad a house is only for a shelter when it rains, or a place to sleep; and a hammock under one of the umbrageous trees is more attractive here than the best bed under a roof. A charcoal brazier and a brass pot, with a few jugs and dishes of coarse pottery, comprise all the household furniture which the coolie needs. Rice and cassava root, with the fruits which are ready at hand, supply their scanty meals. They have little, but their wants are few; they have no debts and no duns; no clothes at the pawnbroker's and very few anywhere; they are accumulating gold and silver pieces to support them for the rest of their lives in Hindustan; they will go home to a blissful Nirvana, or to its equivalent in their simple imaginations.

An agent from "Barnum and Bailey's Greatest Show on Earth" made his appearance while we were at Port of Spain, and engaged passage for a curious collection of Indians from South America, to which he added as stars for the ethnological department of the show, the Hindu priest of the coolie village, and "Julia," a beautiful specimen of a coolie woman. The agent paid these Hindus twenty dollars a month for a six months' trip, and contracted to put them ashore at Trinidad at the end of their contract. They were all deck passengers except Julia, who was allowed a cabin and behaved with as much propriety and conventionality as any of the passengers. The ladies on board were very kind to her, and we were all sorry when she fell into the hands of the reporter

BARBAJEE, HINDU COOLIE PRIEST

who thus exploited the arrival of the *Madiana* in New York:—

"With 'the sword of Adam and Eve' before him and 'the rod of Moses' under his arm, the Right Reverend Barbajee, high priest of the island of Trinidad, descended the gang-plank of the steamer *Madiana* with stately tread yesterday afternoon as she lay alongside the dock of the Quebec Steamship Company. Attired in full sacerdotal robes, with the sacred turban upon his head and a smile of trustfulness upon his genial, ebony countenance, Barbajee has come to convert America through the channel of Barnum and Bailey's peripatetic summer camp-meeting, popularly known as the 'Greatest Show on Earth.' Barbajee was not unattended. Twenty-one men and women and four children from the West Indies and South America came with him on the steamer, under the care of Mr. Bailey's agent. There were five Accawai Indians and four Warrihoones from the Orinoco River, four Caribs, four Hindu Creoles, two Hindus, and three Barbadians in the lot.

"Their many-hued raiment was of the chintz curtain order, but their jewelry was superb. The women were loaded down with bracelets to the elbows, rings on their fingers, and 'bells on their toes.' Ankle rings, earrings, nose rings, and other kinds of ornaments were distributed over every visible portion of their persons, especially the Hindu coolies, of whom there are eighty thousand on the island of Trinidad. There being no law forbidding contract labor there, they are brought over to work on the cocoa plantations under contract, and remain to form an important part of the island's population. The Indians were nearer to nature. Their only ornament was paint, with India ink etching. Their raiment is equally parti-colored but their facial expressions are less engaging. Barbajee is a great evangelist.

"Next to Barbajee, the star of the West Indian combination was Julia Blare Lall. Julia is the belle of Trinidad, and her fortune is her face, and the golden ornaments thereof. Julia talks good English, and though her smile is a little twisted because there are several ounces of gold pendants hanging to her left nostril, she promises to be a success in New York society."

Several of the Indians succumbed to the cold of a New York April, but the others survived. I saw the priest and Julia in the ethnological procession at the Madison Square Garden. They recognized a friendly face and broke ranks to shake hands. It seemed sad to see them marching around the dusty ring in company with a lot of bushmen and barbarians, and I only hope that they will get back to their simple life in the coolie village without disaster. They professed that a desire to see the United States was a more potent motive to make the voyage than the money which was offered them, and judging by my own fondness for new and strange countries, I could not doubt their word.

XXII

LA BREA AND THE PITCH LAKE

WHERE THE PITCH COMES FROM — BLACKNESS OF DARKNESS — TURNING PITCH INTO GOLD — HOMEWARD BOUND — AU REVOIR

SIXTY miles south of Port of Spain is one of the wonders of the world; a dark and disagreeable thing, indeed, but yet a phenomenon. Pitch is no novelty, but a plain of a hundred acres more or less, where the pitch is bubbling up at the rate of tons a day, is certainly worth seeing, and I had no sympathy with the snob who sent his valet to inspect it for him, because, as he said, it was a dirty job and a black lake was not half as beautiful as an ordinary lake. The bitumen deposits by the Dead Sea and at Baku on the Caspian, and the oil wells of Pennsylvania are not beautiful to look upon, but they are curious and instructive, and they promote study and scientific investigation. It was once thought that the Pitch Lake of Trinidad had some connection with the volcanic forces of the West Indies, but a sounder and simpler explanation has been given by practical chemists and surveyors, to wit, that the buried vegetable matter which has been amassed here becomes a sort of peat, and then is converted by the chemical processes of nature into an oily asphalt, which under the pressure of the upper soil gradually oozes up to the surface.

We came to La Brea at daylight in order to avoid the heat, which upon the Pitch Lake in the middle of the day is something frightful. We were put ashore in boats through a heavy surf, landing on a reef of pitch which had flowed down into the sea, and become almost as hard as cement. The beach is mostly covered with black pitch, and a road made artificially of the same material winds up a long but gradual ascent to the lake. The sun had risen, and though the road was partly through woodland, its surface soon became yielding under the heat, and was unpleasantly warm to the feet. It seemed strange to see rich vegetation everywhere, but it is evident that the pitch does not injure it. I picked huge waxy red flowers out of little green oases in the pitchy plain, and a variety of smaller plants and flowers were growing in the same places. But everything was more or less coated with pitch dust, the smell of pitch was in the air, and after a walk of less than a mile up a gentle slope we reached our goal. The black lake with its inky pools, and spots of yellow bubbles, and water cracks, and yielding surface, and strong odor of sulphuretted hydrogen, has been often described, but it must be seen and smelled to be appreciated. Anything more black, malodorous, and repulsive in nature I have never seen upon earth's surface.

It has been likened to a vast asphalt pavement with many furrows and holes filled with inky waters, in which swim ugly fish and black beetles. Charles Kingsley compares it to a crowd of immense black mushrooms of all shapes, close together, their tops on a level, and their rounded rims squeezed tight against each other, with water poured over them so as to fill all the seams. But these are inventions, not descriptions. A vast black lake with multitudes of circles such as are made when a stone is thrown into water, gives a fair idea of the appearance from a little distance. When one comes to walk over the pitch, for it is solid enough to walk over, he finds deep pools and channels of water, and places where the pitch bubbles up with a yellowish scum and a sulphurous smell. If he stands long in one place after the sun is high, his feet sink gradually; and horses and carts which load the material only remain a few moments in the same spot. When pieces of pitch are taken out, nature at once begins to repair the damage, and in twenty-four hours the hole is filled up again. We saw the process beginning in a dozen different places. Besides the curious sight of little islands of rich vegetation rising out of this black plain, there were here and there great pieces of wood sticking up endwise, having apparently come up through the pitch, for they had crowns of pitch on the end which rose two or three feet above the surface. A strange quality of the material was that it did not stick to or soil the hands. I took a ball of the stuff and worked it like putty, and it was not until the water was thoroughly squeezed out that it began to show any dirty or adhesive characteristics. This is due to the amount of earthy matter which is mingled with the vegetable oil in the product.

We walked over acres of the lake, dug into it for specimens, one of the lads caught a fish in a black pool, and lest the sulphuretted hydrogen and the hot sun in combination should make us sick, we limited our visit to about an hour. The tract is leased by the government of Trinidad to an American asphalt company for forty-one years at sixty thousand dollars a year, and the company is coining money. Its president recently paid nearly three-quarters of a million of dollars for a palace in New York, and there is no limit to the business which can be done in this material. It is used for pavements, for roofs, for cellars, for the protection of walls for tombs, for tennis courts and garden paths, for village sidewalks; and new applications are devised every month which will turn this black and ill-smelling mass into the gold which Columbus and his comrades vainly sought in Trinidad. Thus does the world progress, and the discarded and despised materials of one century become the wealth of its successors. The asphalt company has established machinery near the lake to crush and purify the pitch as it comes from the lake in carts, to form it into blocks or pack it in barrels, and an endless chain of huge iron buckets has been set up from the works to the shore to facilitate the transportation of the asphalt to vessels. I was afforded an excellent example to what base uses fine things may come, when I saw the *Madiana*, which was so neat and trim on our winter excursion, lying on a summer day at her New York dock, dirty and grimy, and discharging tons of black freight from La Brea and the Pitch Lake upon the wharf.

We rowed through a rough sea back to our steamer, hoisted the anchor, and before noon were once more at Port of Spain. Our long voyage to the south was ended and the ship was homeward bound.

Over the azure sea, under the Southern Cross, among the beautiful islands whose wonderful symmetry and exquisite outlines had become a constant delight, slipping into the quiet harbors, palm-edged and shadowed by wondrous inland forests, saying "hail and farewell" to friends in the larger towns, so we cruised back to Barbados and Martinique, to Dominica, to Guadeloupe, Antigua and St. Kitt's. We greeted each island as a personality and bade them in turn *au revoir*, for we are sure to come again into this charming region where the winter of our discontent is made glorious summer; where "every prospect pleases," and it is not needful to quote the next line of the good bishop's hymn. If we could only be sure of such agreeable and intelligent companions, and so fortunate a voyage each winter, it would be well to migrate annually like the birds.

One morning we were again at St. Thomas; the men-of-war had departed, the town was asleep; we landed and engaged in commerce; freighted with cigars, bay rum, fruits, and plants, we returned to the ship, and were soon steaming northward. After two days the mercury in the thermometer has fallen to sixty degrees Fahrenheit at noon; there is a chill in the morning air; we steam through floating masses of seaweed; a deep blue water is beneath, and a cold blue and white sky overhead. The passengers have packed up their white clothes and straw hats, and appear in dark tweeds and winter gray suits, with blue yachting caps and black felt hats. West India mangoes and sapodillas have given place to oranges on the table, and we have an appetite for animal food. Ah, a northeaster has struck us; we meet cold, sleety rain; leafless trees; winter lingering in the lap of spring. But we are heartily welcomed home. Some of the warmest and truest of human hearts beat in the colder climates of the earth, and it is our happy lot to have a multitude of such warm-hearted friends. God bless them all.

THE END

A NEW BOOK BY DR. CHARLES A. STODDARD.

CRUISING AMONG THE CARIBBEES

SUMMER DAYS IN WINTER MONTHS.

ILLUSTRATED. 12mo. $1.50.

This new book is a graphic narrative of Dr. Stoddard's experiences and observations during a leisurely cruise among the Windward Islands. The influence of the romantic historical associations of this famed Spanish Main is felt throughout his book; and these pictures of the past bring into relief the author's vivid descriptions of the islands he visited and his racy sketches of the peoples, — English, French, Dutch, Creoles, Coolies, Negroes, and native Caribs, who make up the heterogeneous but infinitely picturesque population. The illustrations, selected from the author's collection, are a real embellishment to the book.

CONTENTS.

I. Literature of the Islands.
II. Discovery and Characteristics.
III. A Sea Change.
IV. The Virgin Group.
V. St. Thomas and its People.
VI. Santa Cruz.
VII. From Saba to St. Kitt's.
VIII. Life on St. Kitt's.
IX. A Real West Indian Island.
X. Antigua and its Annals.
XI. Witchcraft and Superstition.
XII. Guadeloupe.
XIII. Sabbath Day Island.
XIV. Caribs of Dominica and St. Vincent.
XV. Isle de Martinique.
XVI. Battles among the Islands.
XVII. St. Lucia.
XVIII. St. Vincent and the Grenadines.
XIX. Barbados.
XX. Trinidad.
XXI. Hindus at Trinidad.
XXII. La Brea and the Pitch Lake.

DR. STODDARD'S OTHER BOOKS OF TRAVEL.

ACROSS RUSSIA
FROM THE BALTIC TO THE DANUBE.

ILLUSTRATED. 12mo. $1.50.

PRESS NOTICES.

" Dr. Stoddard has all the primary essentials of a tourist, eyes to see, ears to hear, with a well-pronounced faculty of keeping the precious metal separate from the dross. . . . He made good use of his time and of his opportunities, and we but do him justice when we say that we know of no book on the same subject in which so much useful, readable, enjoyable matter is to be found." — *Christian at Work.*

"A most interesting volume. . . . A keen eye, a ready wit, and great felicity of expression have enabled the author to present to the public a book of travels quite out of the ordinary style. While truthful as sober history, it is as charming as a novel." — *New York Journal of Commerce.*

"The volume has many fine illustrations. Mr. Stoddard is a good traveller; he sees well, and his descriptions of people and places are graphic and of large value. . . . Our author takes in all the leading cities, sees what there is to see of art, visits and describes the famous palaces and churches and hospitals, and makes his book as profitable as it is pleasing." — *Chicago Inter-Ocean.*

"In the easy style of a traveller, he tells his readers what is worth telling, and leaves the rest unsaid. . . . The great works of art, the imposing churches, the capacious palaces, all are described in a concise yet satisfactory manner, as well as the customs, religious and otherwise, of the people." — *Christian Intelligencer.*

"The author of this book sets before his readers vivid pictures of this interesting country and people." — *United Presbyterian, Pittsburgh.*

"Mr. Stoddard seems to have had exceptional opportunities to study objects of interest, and writes about them in a way that cannot fail to interest. We have had so many dark pictures of Russia lately that it is a pleasure to get hold of a book that is to a certain degree optimistic. The book is well illustrated." — *The School Journal.*

"The eyes through which we look in this pleasant volume of travels are not unused to sight seeing, and the descriptions here given are entertaining and happy." — *Herald and Presbyter, Cincinnati.*

"The volume richly deserves a place among those welcome helps that are bringing the most distant and unfrequented parts of the earth near to our own doors." — *Golden Rule, Boston.*

BEYOND THE ROCKIES
A SPRING JOURNEY IN CALIFORNIA.

ILLUSTRATED. 12mo. $1.50.

PRESS NOTICES.

"It is a very seductive book, pleasantly written, and draws the reader on with the unfailing and romantic charm of the country." — *The Independent.*

"Dr. Stoddard has written several books of travel, but none more entertaining than this. He had exceptional opportunities for seeing what there is to be seen. The descriptions of life 'Beyond the Rockies' are vivid and fresh beyond what we would consider possible of a land visited by so many travellers. A superb series of photographs illustrate this delightful narrative." — *Philadelphia Ledger.*

"From his long experiences as a traveller he has a faculty of seizing upon what people are likely to want to know, and his account of the wonderful land beyond the Rockies is an uncommonly entertaining book of travel." — *Springfield Republican.*

"Dr. Stoddard writes easily, pleasantly, and often shrewdly of our wonderful Western Coast. There is a good seasoning of fun and incident, and the book is thoroughly readable. It is handsomely illustrated." — *The Outlook.*

"It is not easy to say much that is new of hasty travel in California. But Charles Augustus Stoddard, in 'Beyond the Rockies,' has given to familiar facts and places a new aspect. This was to be looked for from an expert in travel." — *New York Tribune.*

"This prettily illustrated volume is a well-worded series of sketches of a journey from New Orleans to the Pacific Coast, with the incidents of travel, and excellent descriptions of the notable scenes along the way, and the charms of 'the glorious climate' of Southern California. Those who have been there, and seen and enjoyed, will reread the story and enjoy it almost as if it were new." — *Chicago Inter-Ocean.*

"It will be welcomed as a valuable addition to the literature of the great West, most of which is in the necessity of the case obsolete almost as soon as published. From his long experiences as a traveller he has a faculty of seizing upon what people are likely to want to know, and his account of the wonderful land beyond the Rockies is an uncommonly entertaining book of travel, while its language is as enthusiastic as the most ardent Californian could desire." — *Springfield Republican.*

"His style has the merit of freshness; occasionally, indeed, it is illuminated by that special humor which we are in the habit of associating with 'New England seriousness.' But the whole volume is carefully written, and is a conscientious performance in every way." — *Spectator, London.*

SPANISH CITIES
WITH GLIMPSES OF GIBRALTAR AND TANGIER.

ILLUSTRATED. 12mo. $1.50.

PRESS NOTICES.

"He fulfils the ideal of a delightful travelling companion, whose conversation has informing qualities without being tedious, and whose style has sparkle and flavor without froth." — *New York Tribune.*

"His style is direct, easy, and graceful, and his strong English sentences have need of few adjectives to enforce their meaning. His descriptions of places are concise and yet clear, and so markedly elegant as to deserve more than usual commendation." — *Chicago Inter-Ocean.*

"Dr. Stoddard's style is easy and flowing, and he gives us, not merely a chronicle of where he went and what he saw, but he gives us a series of delightful pen pictures of Spain and its people, their habits and customs and modes of life. There are several excellent illustrations which add much to the interest of the work." — *Boston Daily Advertiser.*

"An unusually fresh and beautiful book of travel." — *Brooklyn Daily Eagle.*

"A straightforward, unpretentious, interesting account of travel in Spain, with interesting descriptions of cities, and passing notes of Spanish life without tiresome statistics or historical rehashing." — *The Independent.*

"A writer who has the power of seeing things as well as describing what he sees. To read it is to take one of the most delightful trips conceivable with a charming companion and raconteur. . . . The illustrations are from photographs, and add very much to the attractiveness of the volume." — *The Detroit Free Press.*

"He knows well how to find the points and the persons of special interest, and then understands how to make what interests himself seem vivid and of similar interest to the reader. His style, while pure and simple, is picturesque and easily appeals to the reader's imagination." — *The Advance.*

"Dr. Stoddard is a traveller who knows what he wants to see, and sees it, and a writer who knows how to make his readers see what he has seen. In this pleasant tour in Spain he saw the present and recalled the past, and his sketches of what he saw gain an added touch of romance from the glimpses he gives of what he remembered of their former history." — *The Evangelist.*

CHARLES SCRIBNER'S SONS, Publishers,
743 and 745 BROADWAY, NEW YORK CITY.

www.ingramcontent.com/pod-product-compliance
Lightning Source LLC
Chambersburg PA
CBHW031741230426
43669CB00007B/428